GOD'S BLUEPRINT

FOR THE
GREAT COMMISSION

GEOFFREY COHEN

Geoffrey Cohen
cohen.geoffrey63@gmail.com

Published by

Burkhart Books

Bedford, Texas

PRAISE FOR *GOD'S BLUEPRINT FOR THE GREAT COMMISSION*

I have been friends with Geoffrey Cohen for nearly 15 years. He is one of the most dedicated Jewish evangelists that I know. His heart beats with a passion to share his faith with his people, as well as to educate the Church about God's heart for Israel. *God's Blueprint for the Great Commission* will impact you with God's burden for the world, how to pray for Israel, and how to share your faith more effectively with the Jewish people. May God use the sparks from this book to blaze for the salvation of Israel and the nations!

Wayne Wilks, Jr., Ph.D.
President, Messianic Jewish Bible Institute
Executive Pastor, Jewish Ministry, Gateway Church

CONTENTS

FOREWORD

Geoffrey Cohen makes a compelling case—that those who bless
God's chosen people, the Jews, will be eternally blessed in return.

Geoffrey has been my friend for almost a decade. He's one of
the most gifted evangelists I've witnessed. Geoff's heart beats with
passion for the salvation of Israel. He shares the burden of the great
rabbi, Saul of Tarsus, who cried, "I have great sorrow and continual
grief in my heart . . . for my brethren" (Romans 9:2-3, NKJV) and
". . . my heart's desire and prayer to God for Israel is that they may
be saved" (Romans 10:1, NKJV).

Geoff Cohen has witnessed firsthand the blessings that flow
from "the Jew first" principle. Gateway Church, where Geoffrey
previously led Jewish Ministries, has grown from 30 people in
the year 2000 to nearly 30,000 today. Its multifaceted ministries
are impacting not only the Dallas-Fort Worth metroplex, but
also the globe. Senior Pastor, Robert Morris, attributes much of
Gateway's phenomenal growth and influence to their decision
from the beginning to give firstfruits offerings toward ministry to
the Jew first.

Investing in the future of the Jewish people will eventually
result in huge dividends for the whole world. In the last days the
Jewish people will play a leading role in evangelizing the lost.
In Romans 11:1, Paul reminds us that God has not cast away

His people forever. And their unique calling to be a "light to the nations," (Isaiah 49:6, NASB) will soon resume, "For God's gifts and his call can never be withdrawn" (Romans 11:29, NLT).

Presently, many Jewish people resist the gospel. But this isn't the end of the story. If Paul, who was "breathing threats and murder against the disciples of the Lord" (Acts 9:1, NKJV) eventually answered the Lord's call to "to bear My name before Gentiles, kings, and the children of Israel" (Acts 9:15, NKJV), then surely God is able to re-enlist Paul's Jewish brothers and sisters in their mission to be a light of salvation to the nations in the last days.

Just as the Lord promised to Abraham, that "in you all the families of the earth shall be blessed," (Genesis 12:3, NKJV), so his Jewish offspring will complete their calling to evangelize the world. For the Lord Himself promises, "O house of Judah and house of Israel, so I will save you, and you shall be a blessing" (Zechariah 8:13, NKJV) and "In those days ten men from every language of the nations shall grasp the sleeve of a Jewish man, saying, 'Let us go with you, for we have heard that God is with you.'" (Zechariah 8:23, NKJV) Indeed, the day is coming when Jewish people will ignite a fire of revival. As Paul declared, "Now if their [the Jewish people's] fall *is* riches for the world, and their failure riches for the Gentiles, how much more their fullness!" (Romans 11:12, NKJV) And then three verses later Paul echoes that promise, saying, "For if their *[the Jewish people's]* being cast away *is* the reconciling of the world, what *will* their acceptance *be* but life from the dead?"

Knowing how strategic God's chosen people will be in God's end-time plan, investing in the Jew first is a wise investment. Not only are they a key to worldwide redemption, but also the Jewish people are a key to your blessing here and now. The Lord promised Abraham, "I will bless those who bless you" (Genesis 12:3, NKJV).

Increasingly, churches and individuals are following this millennial-old biblical mandate and are experiencing blessing as a result.

Jesus the Jewish Messiah said to the Gentile woman that, "salvation is from the Jews" (John 4:22, RSV). Gentile Christians owe their very eternal destiny to the Jewish people. And it is for this reason that Paul said the mostly gentile believers in Rome, "For if the Gentiles have been partakers of their spiritual things, their duty is also to minister to them in material things" (Romans 15:27, NKJV).

I personally owe a debt of gratitude to Geoffrey Cohen for his dedication to Israel's spiritual restoration and his spread of the Jew first mandate far and wide. As a result of Geoffrey's efforts, many ministries, along with King of Kings Ministries which I've been privileged to lead in Jerusalem for more than 30 years, have benefitted from an increasing flow of firstfruits offerings of finances, prayer, and manpower.

You're holding in your hands a key to an ancient treasure trove of spiritual riches. Read it cover to cover, like I did, and be blessed!

Wayne Hilsden
Pastor and director of King of Kings Ministries
Jerusalem

ACKNOWLEDGMENTS

Firstly, I thank the God of Abraham, Isaac, and Jacob for sending His Son Jesus, who has saved my soul and given me a new life. Without Him, this book would not be written, and I would have no reason for living.

Secondly, I thank God for my wonderful wife, Tatiana, without whom this revised and updated version would not have happened. She kept on telling me, "though the book is powerful, there is a piece missing." After months of prayer and soul searching, I knew the missing piece was this essential section five on "Bloodguilt."

I also thank my good friend, Manfred Nochomowitz, who read and encouraged me in my new addition.

I thank him and his precious wife, Isit, for being our companions and co-laborers in Jewish ministry. I also want to thank our incredible friends Dr. Cynthia Shinabarger Reed and her husband, Dr. Robert Reed, for helping me with editing my new additions as well as being such invaluable partners and friends in the ministry and life.

I give a big "thank you" to Laura Wilson for her help in editing and the invaluable friendship of her and her husband, Ronny, to us.

Special thanks to Rudolph and Betsy Claasen for being such a beacon of light and support for us.

We also thank our very special friends, Aharon and Zhenya Mendez, for always being there for us.

There are many other brothers and sisters in the Lord, too numerous to mention, who have supported us and pray for us regularly. A big "thank you" to you all.

INTRODUCTION

Our God is a God of order. He has a pattern for almost everything. Each star remains in its place in the heavens. The seasons always occur in the same order and transition smoothly. The birds know when to migrate from one climate to another to survive, and bears know when it is time to hibernate before the onset of winter.

But what about the patterns God instituted for the human race? How do we know what His plans are for us? The answer is simple. He provided His plan for our lives in His Book, called the Bible. We were born in sin and He sent His Son, Jesus, to deliver us from an eternity separated from Him. His death on the cross, and His subsequent burial and resurrection, delivered us from death and hell forever. More than that, He came to give us an abundant life on this earth (John 10:10), even though we all suffer the common trials of humanity because we live in a fallen world.

In the Scriptures, God teaches us how to live our lives, how to love one another, and how to exist in harmony with our fellow man. He tells us how to prosper in marriage, how to raise our children, and how to handle our finances. He also tells us what is right and wrong. If we do what is wrong, He convicts us by His Holy Spirit and prompts us in the right direction so we can improve as people and continue to grow in our relationship with Him and with one another.

The message God has given us about His Son's redemption is called the gospel. He has instructed all believers to share this message with the rest of mankind because it is the only hope for our redemption. It is not just one option of deliverance from the consequences of sin through the fall of Adam and Eve in the garden. It is the only long-term solution for the human race. And it is ultimately the only way to enjoy life after death.

I believe the gospel is the most underrated and underappreciated message on the planet, and most of us do not take it as seriously as we should. I daresay, it is the best-kept secret of the church! Surely that can't be pleasing to God, who sacrificed the most precious thing He had, His one and only Son, for us.

God has entrusted this incredible, one-of-a-kind message to believers in Jesus. He wants us to take it into all the world and to share it with every person we know in a way that is understandable for them. And God, who has a pattern for everything in the universe, has an order for how we are to share that message.

In this book we will study the biblical pattern God has set in place for the most effective way to bring the gospel to the whole human race. The first-century disciples followed this method and were so successful that the world was forever changed, and time was separated between BC and AD from that point on.

What was the secret of their effectiveness? What did they do that we are missing? Why were they so successful in a time without the Internet, social media, and instant communication such as we have today? How could they reach the entire known world using what we would consider basic, primitive methods, traveling mostly on foot in pairs, preaching the gospel?

They followed a pattern that God gave them, and the results have never been truly replicated. Until now! Some people today are beginning to rediscover this ancient method, demonstrated throughout the Scriptures, and they are using it with great results and abundant fruit.

What is this pattern? Romans 1:16 (NIV) says it is to bring the gospel "first to the Jew, then to the Gentile."

The people at Gateway Church in Southlake, Texas, a congregation of about thirty-nine thousand, are following this pattern. As a result they have seen supernatural numerical growth and unprecedented financial blessing. Other churches are also tapping into this plan for fulfilling the Great Commission and are experiencing the same blessings.

In this book, we will look at this pattern and analyze the reasons God set it in place. We will also consider why this is the method God blesses the most.

Even though great blessings follow those who bring the gospel to the Jewish people, in the end it is not about us being blessed but rather about us being a blessing to others. There is no greater gift we can give to the Jewish people than the gift of eternal life through their promised Messiah.

As you read this book, you will see why we are to follow the pattern of "to the Jew first." You will also be given practical tools to use and steps you can take to personally bring your Jewish friends and neighbors to the Lord. These methods have enabled me to lead countless Jewish people to faith in God through their Messiah. After reading this book, you too will be equipped to be a blessing to the Jewish people in your life.

Part One

Why to the Jew First?

Even though the principle of taking the gospel to the Jew first was well established as one of the foundational principles of the early New Testament church, many Christians today are not very familiar with it. So I am going to spend a significant portion of this book dealing with its systematic theological foundation.

Please understand up front that the gospel is not *only* for the Jews. Nor is it favoritism or preferential treatment to take the gospel to the Jew first. Rather, it is a matter of divine order. God loves the whole world, and He knows that this is the most effective method for the gospel to reach everyone.

Just because the biblical pattern is to take the gospel to the Jew first, that doesn't mean that you can't preach the gospel to any Gentiles until you find a Jew to share with. "To the Jew first" is a biblical principle, not a law. Following it should be a joy, not a burden. It has been a delight and a blessing to me for almost three decades, and that's what I hope to bring to others as well.

Below are nine biblical reasons the gospel is "to the Jew first." There are many more examples in Scripture, but for the sake of brevity and clarity, I will emphasize these nine.

REASON #1. IT IS THE BIBLICAL PATTERN

God is a God of order and logic. Some would say that faith defies logic, but I beg to differ. It's true that we often can't understand God's methods, but that's because His ways are much higher than ours and His thoughts much deeper than ours (Isaiah 55:9). We are not the source of all logic and order—He is. The creation is not more intelligent than the Creator. God is orderly and logical in everything He does, even if we don't always understand His reasoning.

God has a pattern for the order of the entire universe: the stars, the sun, the moon. The Earth rotates consistently at the same speed on the same axis and remains at the perfect distance from the sun to create life and growth. If it were any closer, it would burn up; any farther and it would freeze over. Volumes of books could be written on how maintaining nature's perfect balance is crucial for animal species to survive. Sadly, man has destroyed the intricate balance of many ecosystems and broken the patterns established in nature for its survival. As a result, many species are now extinct and our children will not be able to enjoy all that past generations did.

God cares about everything He created, but He cares most about people. Jesus said that not even one sparrow falls out of the sky apart from His will, and how much more will he care for people, who are worth far more than many sparrows because we are made in His image (Matthew 10:29–31).

Our loving heavenly Father sacrificed the most precious gift He had for you and me. "God demonstrates His own love for us, in that while we were still sinners, Christ died for us" (Romans 5:8). But God's care did not end when Jesus died. He now wants us to get the message of this glorious gospel into all the world.

God has placed this monumental responsibility into our hands. If I were God, I would never trust fallible mankind with such a crucial task. (Thankfully, I am not God—nor do I aspire to be!)

As a new Jewish believer, I was filled with awe and wonder at the incredible redemption I was experiencing. Everything in the world seemed fresh, crisp, and new. I felt truly alive for the first time, excited and motivated about my life and my destiny. I felt connected to God and filled with love, peace, and joy like I had never known. And I knew that when I died, I would go straight into the arms of my loving Father. I never had to fear death again.

But a distressing question nagged at my heart. Why had no Christians told me that the Messiah had come? After all, Jews had been cut off from the gospel for almost two thousand years. How could the Christians have kept this to themselves all this time? Didn't they know Jesus was the only hope for my people? This mystery rankled my soul.

My anger gradually evolved into a sense of mission and purpose. I was determined to do whatever I could to encourage and empower Christians to share with all their Jewish friends that the Jewish Messiah has come. That is what I've been doing for the last three decades, and I will continue to do it until I go to be with the Lord.

As wonderful as God's redemption plan is, no will know about it unless we tell them. And God has a pattern for how we are to go about tackling this crucial task. According to Romans 1:16 (NIV), that pattern is "first to the Jew, then to the Gentile."

REASON #2. IT IS GOD'S BLUEPRINT FOR HIS LIVING TABERNACLE

God had a divine blueprint for the tabernacle He instructed Moses to build. He gave him specific instructions as to the dimensions and the materials to be used, right down to the finest detail. These specifics were so important to God that He repeated the instructions.

In Exodus 25:9 (NIV), God said, "Make this tabernacle and all its furnishings exactly like the pattern I will show you." In verse 40 of the same chapter, He reiterated the point. "See that you make them according to the pattern shown you on the mountain" (NIV).

Exodus 25:10–15 (NIV) gives us a peek at how specific God was with some of the minutiae of the details of one part of this tabernacle: the ark.

> Have them make an ark of acacia wood—two and a half cubits long, a cubit and a half wide, and a cubit and a half high. Overlay it with pure gold, both inside and out, and make a gold molding around it. Cast four gold rings for it and fasten them to its four feet, with two rings on one side and two rings on the other. Then make poles of acacia wood and overlay them with gold. Insert the poles into the rings on the sides of the ark to carry it. The poles are to remain in the rings of this ark; they are not to be removed.

That is a lot of detail, and it's just the beginning. If you read the whole chapter, you might find it a bit boring, but God had a reason for providing so much detail.

It's not that God has an obsessive-compulsive disorder or that He suffers from short-term memory loss because He has been around for so long. God gave such precise instructions because there is a tabernacle in heaven, and He wanted the one on earth to be an exact replica of it.

Since Moses could not see the one in heaven, God had to make the instructions extremely clear.

How do you think God would have felt if Moses had said, "Lord, I appreciate your attention to detail and all, but gold is really rare out here in the desert, and silver will work just fine. Acacia wood is also very rare. In fact, all wood is rare out here. But we brought some pine wood from Egypt with us. I think we should use that instead"?

I can tell you, God would not have been happy about that at all. If Moses had used any other materials, or if he'd gotten the dimensions wrong, the earthly tabernacle would not have been an exact replica of the one in heaven.

> When Moses had proclaimed every command of the law to all the people, he took the blood of calves, together with water, scarlet wool and branches of hyssop, and sprinkled the scroll and all the people. He said, "This is the blood of the covenant, which God has commanded you to keep." In the same way, he sprinkled with the blood both the tabernacle and everything used in its ceremonies. In fact, the law requires that nearly everything be cleansed with blood, and without the shedding of blood there is no forgiveness.
>
> It was necessary, then, for *the copies of the heavenly things* to be purified with these sacrifices, but the heavenly things themselves with better sacrifices than these (Hebrews 9:19–23 NIV, emphasis added).

The "copies of the heavenly things" referred to in this passage include the earthly tabernacle Moses built. It had to be an exact replica of the tabernacle in heaven so as not to misrepresent God in any way.

God's Blueprint for His Living Tabernacle

God also has a precise pattern for building His living tabernacle on earth. He does not want us to be haphazard about the way we build His body here. He is a God of order, and nothing He does is unintentional.

According to Scripture, God's new tabernacle is you and me and all believers on this planet. "We know that if our earthly house *of this tabernacle* were dissolved, we have a building of God, an house not made with hands, eternal in the heavens" (2 Corinthians 5:1 KJV, emphasis added). Verse 4 adds, "We that are *in this tabernacle* do groan, being burdened: not for that we would be unclothed, but clothed upon, that mortality might be swallowed up of life"

(KJV, emphasis added). Individually, each of us is His tabernacle. And collectively, we are being built to become His holy temple on earth.

If God has an exact plan for the building of His earthly tabernacle made of wood and precious metals, surely He is even more concerned about the plan for the building of His living tabernacle on earth, made up of those who are created in His image. He is deeply concerned about us being effective in reaching the world with His message.

God's method, as established in Romans 1:16 and throughout the New Testament, is to take the gospel to the Jew first and then to the Gentile. That is the most fruitful and successful way to reach the maximum number of people in the shortest amount of time. "To the Jew first" is His pattern, so that is what He will bless the most.

REASON #3. IT WAS JESUS' PERSONAL PATTERN

As believers, we want to follow Jesus' example in everything He did. In His personal ministry, He lived out and demonstrated the principle of going to the Jew first. This is most clearly demonstrated in His interaction with the Canaanite woman in Matthew 15.

After ministering to the Jews in Genesaret, Jesus left that region and headed toward Tyre and Sidon. Sidon was a Phoenician city that had been a Canaanite stronghold for centuries. This area had long been a thorn in the flesh to Israel, especially during the period of the judges (Judges 10:12). Once Israel was established in the land, many of the Jews began to worship the gods of the Sidonians, principally Baal and Ashtoreth, the goddess of fertility. Ethbaal, the king of Sidon and father of Jezebel (1 Kings 16:31), was primarily responsible for introducing pagan gods into Israel.

The Jews and the Canaanites had been sworn enemies for centuries. The animosity between the two groups could be compared to that between Israelis and Palestinians in modern times. Yet after preaching to the Jews in the Galilee region, this was right where Jesus headed.

When He arrived in Sidon, a Canaanite woman from the area approached Jesus. This would have been quite surprising, since He was a Jew and was surrounded by His disciples, who were also Jews. They would have been able to tell by the way this woman dressed that she was not Jewish. When she spoke, her accent and pronunciation would have immediately identified her as a Canaanite. The disciples must have wondered what she was about to do or say.

In fact, she did do something unexpected. She cried out to Jesus, "Have mercy on me, O Lord, Son of David! My daughter is severely demon-possessed" (Matthew 15:22).

For a Canaanite woman to approach a Jewish man was bizarre enough. But then she called Him Lord. She had no way of knowing about Jesus' deity, so most likely she meant to call Him "Master." On top of that, she referred to Him as "Son of David," a commonly accepted messianic term in that time. We can only speculate as to why she would call Him that, because many of His own disciples did not yet fully realize that He was the Messiah.

When Jesus had asked the disciples who they thought He was, Peter was the only one who answered correctly, saying that He was "the Messiah, the Son of God" (John 11:27 NIV). He said this by revelation of the Holy Spirit. Could it be that the Holy Spirit supernaturally revealed to this pagan woman who Jesus was so that her daughter could be healed?

Canaanite or not, she must have had a heart for God, as she was drawn to His Son. She had probably heard rumors that Jesus could heal the sick, and so she approached Him. I sometimes wonder if desperation in a time of need is a prerequisite for revelation. It certainly seems to be in this case.

The disciples waited to see how Jesus would respond. For any woman to approach a man was considered taboo in those days. And interaction with a Canaanite would make a Jew ceremonially unclean.

Then again, much to the disciples' disdain, Jesus had once told a Samaritan woman that He could give her living water if she believed in Him (John 4:9). He had even healed Gentiles, at times actually commending them for their great faith. On one occasion, Jesus told a Roman centurion, "I have not found such great faith, *not even in Israel!*" (Matthew 8:10, emphasis added).

And yet, Jesus ignored this Canaanite woman. "He answered her not a word" (Matthew 15:23). The disciples immediately jumped on the bandwagon and urged Him to send her away. They considered her to be irritating and an inconvenience to their peaceful day. They were not moved with compassion for this pagan woman, in spite of her anguish over her demon-possessed daughter.

The disciples could have sent her away themselves. But they never knew how Jesus was going to respond in any given situation. They probably didn't want to hear another sharp rebuke from Jesus, like the Sons of Thunder got when they asked Him if they should call down fire from heaven because the Samaritans would not let them pass through their village (Luke 9:54). They were beginning to notice a pattern in Jesus' reaching out to Gentiles as well as to Jews. So they played it safe this time and asked Him to send her away.

But in her desperation, she persisted in crying out to Him. Again the disciples waited for Jesus' response. This time He said to her, "I was not sent except to the lost sheep of the house of Israel" (Matthew 15:24).

This was not meant to be harsh in any way. Jesus was merely declaring the calling the Father had entrusted to Him for His earthly ministry. God had called Him primarily to minister to His own people, the Jews—who, because of their spiritual condition at the time, He referred to as "the lost sheep of the house of Israel."

Finally Jesus was saying what the disciples had hoped He would. They must have figured the woman would leave Him alone now. But she was undeterred. This doting and caring mother was not going to accept no for an answer, even from the Son of David. What a great lesson in persistence for us all.

She prostrated herself before Jesus in worship and cried out, probably even louder this time, "Lord, help me!" (v. 25).

The disciples must have thought this pagan was going overboard and getting obnoxious. They watched carefully to see how Jesus would respond to this pesky, determined woman.

Jesus answered her, "It is not good to take the children's bread and throw it to the little dogs" (v. 26). The "children" He referred to here were the sons of Abraham (the Jews). Bread was a reference to healing. The Jews in those days commonly used *dog* as a derogatory term for a Gentile because they were idol worshippers and ceremonially unclean according to Jewish law.

Jesus' response must have surprised the disciples, because that was probably how they wanted to reply. Even though He was speaking matter-of-factly, His comment bordered on insult.

Of course, Jesus did not intend it that way. He was merely stating a fact about His calling. The Father had sent Him to bring deliverance and healing to the Jewish nation as their Messiah, even though He brought it in a way they did not expect.

Nowhere else in all four Gospels do we find any other account where Jesus refused to heal anyone because he or she wasn't Jewish.

How would this woman respond now that Jesus had made it clear that His ministry was to the Jews and that healing was also for the Jews? Surely at last she would leave Him alone and the disciples could be relieved of this pesky female.

But no. She refused to give up until she received what she came for. This woman knew Jesus was her only hope. If He did not grant her request, her child would never be set free. Somehow she understood that Jesus alone had the power to drive the demons out of her daughter.

"Yes, Lord," she said, "yet even the little dogs eat the crumbs which fall from their master's table" (v. 27).

Jesus answered, "O woman, great is your faith! Let it be to you as you desire."

This must have been a slap in the face to the disciples. After all, they had descended directly from Abraham, the father of the faith.

Matthew 15:28 tells us, "Her daughter was healed from that very hour." I believe Jesus fully intended to heal that little girl the very first time her mother asked. Jesus always had a heart for all mankind, including the Gentiles, and it was always His intention to touch and to heal anyone who asked in faith.

So why did He resist this woman's request four times before He finally healed her daughter? I believe He wanted all generations who would ever read the Bible to know that His primary calling during His earthly ministry in the flesh was to the Jewish people, even though He also healed Gentiles. This story reflects God's blueprint for bringing the gospel to the world: "first to the Jew, then to the Gentile."

And we are called to emulate Jesus as our ultimate example.

REASON #4. IT WAS THE APOSTLES' COMMISSION

Jesus passed this mandate on to the original twelve apostles.

> When He had called His twelve disciples to Him, He gave them power over unclean spirits, to cast them out, and to heal all kinds of sickness and all kinds of disease. . . .These twelve Jesus sent out and commanded them, saying: "Do not go into the way of the Gentiles, and do not enter a city of the Samaritans. But go rather to the lost sheep of the house of Israel. And as you go, preach, saying, 'The kingdom of heaven is at hand.'" (Matthew 10:1–7).

Jesus gave the newly appointed apostles power over unclean spirits. Then He instructed the Twelve where *not* to go. First He told them *not to go to the Gentiles*. Then He added that they were *not to go to the Samaritans*.

Many people ignore this text because they think it shows favoritism—that somehow God favors Jews over Gentiles and thus offers them preferential treatment. But Scripture clearly points out that "God does not show favoritism" (Romans 2:11 NIV).

God loves all people equally. That is why John 3:16 says, "God so loved the *world* that He gave His only begotten Son, that whoever believes in Him should not perish but have everlasting life" (emphasis added). Favoritism is identified as a sin in the book of James (2:9), and we know that Jesus never sinned.

Part of the problem with interpreting biblical texts today is that we tend to view them within the context of contemporary living. In the twenty-first century, *Gentiles* refers to anyone who is not a Jew by heritage or belief system. In the US, this would include Baptists, Methodists, Presbyterians, Catholics, etc., whether or not they are faithful church attenders. In the New Testament, however, the term *Gentiles* referred to ungodly pagans. When these texts were written, the church was made up almost exclusively of Jewish believers, so there was no such thing as a Gentile church.

Why Not to the Gentiles?

Why was Jesus so emphatic that the apostles were not to bring the gospel to the Gentiles?

In those days Gentiles worshipped a plethora of Greek and Roman gods, including Zeus and Apollos. They built temples to many of their gods. For example, an entire religion was devoted solely to the fertility goddess, Aphrodite. Temple prostitution went on there, as well as human sacrifice, orgies, and other horrible things.

Jesus told the disciples not to preach the gospel to them because they already believed in many gods. If they heard the gospel, Jesus would have merely been added to their pantheon. At best, we would have ended up with a watered-down version of the gospel. Or worse, we might have lost the gospel message completely, because no one would have bothered creating a verifiable written account of Jesus' death on the cross as a fulfillment of the Law and the Prophets. Only a Jew could record that accurately, because the Scriptures were given to the Jews and written by Jews. They alone understood that anyone who claimed to be the Messiah had to fulfill the Old Testament prophecies.

If these details had not been recorded by the Jewish believers of that day, Jesus' sacrifice would have been in vain, because future generations would never know about it.

Jesus' followers went to great pains to write their accounts with accurate detail, carefully recording every fulfillment of the Old Testament prophecies. If they hadn't done this, we would not possess what we know today as the New Testament. Nor would we have the incredible privilege of experiencing the salvation that is available to all, for which we are so grateful.

Jesus did not tell the apostles to avoid taking the gospel to the Gentiles because He didn't love them, but *because He does love them.* He told the apostles to bring the message to the Jews first so they would have access to the pure, full gospel of salvation, as promised in the messianic prophecies of the Old Testament, which could then be passed on to others.

Why Not to the Samaritans?

Why did Jesus say specifically not to take the gospel to the Samaritans?

Many of the Samaritans were half Jewish. They claimed a strong Jewish heritage, but they had some different ideas than the Jews did about how and where to worship.

When Jesus met the Samaritan woman at the well, she noted some of the stark contrasts between Jewish worship and Samaritan worship. For one thing, the Samaritans did not recognize the temple in Jerusalem as the center of worship. They believed God wanted people to worship on Mount Gerizim (currently the West Bank, by the city of Nablus). Even to this day the Samaritans believe that the original temple was on Mount Gerizim, even though the Old Testament clearly states it was in Jerusalem. Archaeological excavations of the Western Wall, including the remaining stairs leading to the temple, back that up.

The Samaritans of today also consider themselves part Jewish. But they still have notable differences in their belief systems. For example, they do not recognize all of the accepted canon of the

Old Testament. They believe that only the five books written by Moses (Genesis through Deuteronomy) and the book of Joshua are the inspired Word of God. They also have their own version of the book of Joshua, which neither Jews nor Christians recognize as part of the canonical texts.

If Jesus had allowed the gospel to go to the Samaritans first, we would have ended up with a hybrid version of the message, interpreted through their alternate belief system and worldview. And the center of worship would have been Mount Gerizim instead of Jerusalem.

Why to the Jews First?

Unlike Gentiles or Samaritans, the Jews had the foundation of the Law and the Prophets. They had all of the messianic prophecies at their disposal. And some of them knew why the Messiah had to come and what He would do.

When King Herod wanted to know where the Messiah was to be born, he did not waste his time asking Samaritans or Gentiles. He went straight to the leaders of the Jews, who knew and understood the prophecies because they were written by Jews. They told him that the Messiah was to be born in Bethlehem and would be from the tribe of Judah (Matthew 2:2–6).

Jesus knew that ultimately it would serve the world best if the gospel was presented to the Jews first, as they would understand the context of the message. Because the apostles obeyed Jesus' instructions and went directly to the Jews with the gospel, we have the complete Scriptures available to us today. Jesus' disciples understood the Old Testament and incessantly referred to the Law and the Prophets, using phrases like "It is written" or "As it is written."

Some Christians only read the New Testament. Even some pastors do not preach from the Old Testament. But the Old Testament prophecies described who the Messiah would be, down to the finest details. That is how the early Jewish believers were able to identify Jesus as the promised Messiah. Both portions of the Scriptures are equally important, as each one is the inspired Word of God.

It is impossible to understand the New Testament without the Old. Anyone who hasn't read the Old Testament hasn't really read the Bible, because roughly a third of the New Testament either quotes from the Old Testament or explains what the Old Testament prophecies are referring to. The Old Testament points forward to the New Testament. The New Testament points back to and explains the Old Testament. And the cross weaves them both together into an eternal tapestry that paints a picture of forgiveness and salvation to the whole world.

REASON #5. IT WAS PASSED ON TO THE APOSTLES PAUL AND PETER

The pattern of taking the gospel to the Jew first did not stop with the twelve disciples. The Holy Spirit passed on this established pattern to the apostle Paul. Although he was called to be "the apostle to the Gentiles," taking the gospel to the Jew first was one of the hallmarks of Paul's ministry. I believe the reason his ministry to the Gentiles was so successful was that he obediently followed God's pattern of taking the gospel to the Jew first and then to the Gentile.

In Romans 1:16 (NIV), Paul wrote, "I am not ashamed of the gospel, because it is the power of God that brings salvation to everyone who believes: first to the Jew, then to the Gentile." We would all say a resounding "Amen!" to the fact that the gospel is the power of God for salvation for everyone who believes. But we tend to ignore the last half of that verse because we don't know what to do with it. However, just because something in Scripture might be inconvenient, or we don't know how it fits into our theology, that doesn't mean we should ignore it.

So let's see how Paul, on his missionary journeys to the Gentiles, followed the principle of taking the gospel to the Jew first.

In the church at Antioch there were prophets and teachers: Barnabas,
Simeon called Niger, Lucius of Cyrene, Manaen (who had been brought
up with Herod the tetrarch) and Saul. While they were worshiping the
Lord and fasting, the Holy Spirit said, "Set apart for me Barnabas and
Saul for the work to which I have called them." So after they had fasted
and prayed, they placed their hands on them and sent them off.

The two of them, sent on their way by the Holy Spirit, went down
to Seleucia and sailed from there to Cyprus. *When they arrived at
Salamis, they proclaimed the word of God in the Jewish synagogues*
(Acts 13:1–5 NIV, emphasis added).

Even though Barnabas and Paul (called Saul in this text) were
on the Greek island of Cyprus in the city of Salamis, they made
a conscious effort to seek out the Jewish community first, which
in those days always gathered around the synagogue. Paul shared
the gospel with these Jews, using the Old Testament messianic
prophecies as his foundation.

Paul and Barnabas then traveled to what is present-day
Turkey and followed the same pattern. From Perga they went on
to Pisidian Antioch. On the Sabbath they entered the synagogue.
After reading from the Law and the Prophets, the rulers of the
synagogue asked them if they had any message of encouragement
for the people.

Paul stood and addressed his audience, comprised of Jews and
God-fearing Gentiles.

Fellow Israelites and you Gentiles who worship God, listen to me! The
God of the people of Israel chose our ancestors; he made the people
prosper during their stay in Egypt; with mighty power he led them
out of that country; for about forty years he endured their conduct in
the wilderness; and he overthrew seven nations in Canaan, giving their
land to his people as their inheritance. All this took about 450 years.

After this, God gave them judges until the time of Samuel the
prophet. Then the people asked for a king, and he gave them Saul son

of Kish, of the tribe of Benjamin, who ruled forty years. After remov-
ing Saul, he made David their king. God testified concerning him:
"I have found David son of Jesse, a man after my own heart; he will
do everything I want him to do."

From this man's descendants God has brought to Israel the Savior
Jesus, as he promised (Acts 13:16–23 NIV).

Notice that Paul began with the history of the Jewish people,
starting with their deliverance from Egypt and their coming into
the Promised Land. He then shared how God brought them their
greatest king, David, a man after God's own heart. He concluded
by stating that through David's lineage, God ultimately brought
the Jews their promised Messiah.

As a result of this powerful message, many Jews and Gentiles
became followers of the Lord. In fact, the people were so moved
by what Paul said that they invited him and Barnabas back to the
synagogue the next Sabbath, and "almost the whole city gathered
to hear the word of the Lord" (v. 44 NIV).

How exciting would it be if an entire city came to hear the
Word of God today!

By following the pattern of going to the Jew first, Paul reached
a multitude of Gentiles. He knew that the key to reaching the
Gentiles most effectively was to follow God's divine blueprint and
then trust Him to take care of the results.

On the first Sabbath that Paul and Barnabas preached, many
Jews were saved. But when they returned to preach to the packed-
out synagogue, some Jewish antagonists showed up who were
jealous of the large crowds Paul and Barnabas were drawing. They
heckled them and spoke against what they were doing, trying to
disrupt the meeting.

Paul and Barnabas answered them boldly:

We had to speak the word of God to you first. Since you reject it and
do not consider yourselves worthy of eternal life, we now turn to the
Gentiles. For this is what the Lord has commanded us: "I have made
you a light for the Gentiles, that you may bring salvation to the ends

of the earth." When the Gentiles heard this, they were glad and honored the word of the Lord; and all who were appointed for eternal life believed (Acts 13:46–48 NIV).

Unfortunately, some people read about this frustrated moment in Paul's ministry and conclude that God became fed up with the Jews as a nation at this point, and from that time onward, Paul abandoned taking the gospel to the Jew first. But that's not the case.

Taking a verse of Scripture out of context and creating a doctrine out of it is highly dangerous. So let's look closely at whom Paul was speaking to, and whom he said he would preach the gospel to.

When Paul said, "Since you reject it and do not consider yourselves worthy of eternal life, we now turn to the Gentiles," he was addressing just a handful of Jews who were heckling him at this meeting. Because they rejected him, he brought the message to the Gentiles who were present at the time, and then to other Gentiles in the future.

The persecution that resulted from these hecklers stirring up the masses against Paul and Barnabas was so fierce that they had to leave that place and go to Iconium, a huge, mostly Gentile city. On the very next Sabbath, Paul and Barnabas "went *as usual* into the Jewish synagogue" (Acts 14:1 NIV, emphasis added). This was their normal mode of operation as they traveled throughout Europe and Asia, preaching the gospel.

Paul's preaching in the synagogue at Iconium was so effective that "a great number of Jews and Greeks believed" (Acts 14:1 NIV).

Paul continued to follow this pattern of preaching to the Jew first. He never strayed from it throughout his whole ministry. And God blessed his ministry to the Gentiles immensely as a result of his obedience.

Peter

In the first century, one of the biggest questions among Jewish believers was "Is the gospel for Jews only, or is it also for the Gentiles?" Ironically, we often ask the opposite question today.

God gave Peter the answer to this question in an astonishing way.

> Peter went up on the housetop to pray, about the sixth hour. Then he
> became very hungry and wanted to eat; but while they made ready,
> he fell into a trance and saw heaven opened and an object like a great
> sheet bound at the four corners, descending to him and let down to
> the earth. In it were all kinds of four-footed animals of the earth, wild
> beasts, creeping things, and birds of the air. And a voice came to him,
> "Rise, Peter; kill and eat."
>
> But Peter said, "Not so, Lord! For I have never eaten anything
> common or unclean."
>
> And a voice spoke to him again the second time, "What God has
> cleansed you must not call common." This was done three times. And
> the object was taken up into heaven again (Acts 10:9–16).

While Peter was still pondering the meaning of the vision,
three Gentiles approached him. They had been sent by Cornelius,
a Roman centurion, to ask if he would come and speak to him.
They told Peter, "A holy angel told him to ask you to come to his
house so that he could hear what you have to say" (v. 22 NIV).

Considering the astonishing amount of supernatural activ-
ity in visions and angelic appearances, first to a Jew and then to a
Roman centurion, God must have had a very important message
to bring through Peter to the Gentiles. But what could it be?

Peter invited the three men to stay with him overnight. The
next day he headed out with them and some of his Jewish breth-
ren to Caesarea, where Cornelius lived—a two-day journey from
Joppa, where Peter lived. When the entourage finally arrived at
Cornelius's house, they discovered that he had invited all of his
closest relatives and friends to hear what Peter was going to say.
"We are all here in the presence of God to listen to everything the
Lord has commanded you to tell us" (v. 33 NIV), he said.

I am sure you could have heard a pin drop as they waited anx-
iously to hear what Peter was about to say. And his first sentence

was a bombshell. "I now realize how true it is that God does not show favoritism but accepts from every nation the one who fears him and does what is right" (vv. 34–35 NIV).

Peter went on to preach the gospel with great power and authority, and while he was speaking, the Holy Spirit fell on all who were listening (v. 44). Then "the circumcised believers who had come with Peter *were astonished* that the gift of the Holy Spirit had been poured out even on Gentiles. For they heard them speaking in tongues and praising God" (vv. 45–46 NIV, emphasis added).

The Jewish believers were shocked to see Gentiles getting saved and receiving the Holy Spirit. They thought the gospel was only for the Jewish people. It wasn't that they disliked Gentiles or were prejudiced toward them. But their understanding of the ancient prophecies was that the Messiah would come to save and redeem the Jews. It took divine revelation for God to show them that the gospel is for all people, both Jews and Gentiles.

Because of this revelation to Peter and Paul, the Jewish believers began to take the gospel to the Gentiles as well as the Jews. The Gentiles have run with the gospel for about two thousand years, making what we know today as Christianity the largest religion in the world. Millions of Gentiles have been swept into the kingdom and have entered into a personal relationship with the God of Abraham as a result of Paul's divine revelation of Jesus on the road to Damascus and the vision Peter received while on the roof of his house in Joppa, followed by the angelic visitations.

In the first century, it came as a huge surprise to the Jewish believers to find out that the gospel is not for the Jews only. Today we struggle to believe that the gospel is "first to the Jew, then to the Gentile." In fact, Gentiles are often astounded to meet a Jew who believes in Jesus. But times are changing, and Jews are beginning to come back to their God through the realization that Yeshua (Jesus' Hebrew name) is the promised and prophesied Messiah of Israel.

It's time to take the gospel back to those through whom it came. Isn't that the least we can do to show our gratitude to the Jewish believers who first brought the gospel to the Gentile world, often at the cost of their very lives?

REASON #6. ISRAEL IS GOD'S FIRSTBORN

In today's world, being the firstborn is not as significant as it was in biblical times. But the firstborn is so important to the Lord that God commanded Moses to consecrate the firstborn of both man and beast to Him (Exodus 13:2). The firstborn is considered holy to the Lord.

The principle of the firstborn is mentioned 141 times in Scripture. In ancient Israel the firstborn son inherited a double portion of the estate. Upon the father's passing, the firstborn son usually inherited the patriarchal role over the family, much as the son of a king would inherit the throne and all the rights and privileges that come with it. He also inherited the priestly role in terms of the spiritual headship over the family.

That is why it was such a big deal when Jacob stole the birthright of the firstborn from Esau (Genesis 25:33). Later, when Jacob prophesied over his sons, he called his firstborn, Reuben, "my might and the beginning of my strength, the excellency of dignity and the excellency of power" (Genesis 49:3).

Usually the term *firstborn* refers to a person or an animal that opens the womb. But we see an exception to this rule when God refers to Israel. He calls the whole nation His firstborn.

When God spoke to Moses before he went to Egypt, He gave him instructions about what to do to secure the release of His people. God told him to tell Pharaoh on His behalf, "Israel is my firstborn son, and I told you, 'Let my son go, so he may worship me.' But you refused to let him go; so I will kill your firstborn son" (Exodus 4:22–23).

God said this to Moses before the beginning of the ten plagues, which culminated in the death of the firstborn sons of Egypt. God knew in advance that Pharaoh would harden his heart.

Is it possible that Christians today are hardening their hearts to the Jews by refusing to let God's firstborn go, as Pharaoh did, so they can worship Him? You may not think this is possible. But many Christians are withholding the gospel from the Jews by not letting their Jewish friends and neighbors know that the only way they can worship the God of their fathers is through Jesus, their Messiah.

The firstborn represented the strength of Egypt and the strength of Pharaoh, which God determined to bring down as a result of the mistreatment of the Jews and for refusing to let them go so they could worship God freely.

God prophesied the demise of the Egyptian nation when He made His covenant with Abraham. "Know for certain that for four hundred years your descendants will be strangers in a country not their own and that they will be enslaved and mistreated there. But I will punish the nation they serve as slaves, and afterward they will come out with great possessions" (Genesis 15:13–14 NIV).

Though God allowed the Jews to be enslaved in Egypt after Joseph died, He had already determined that He was going to judge Egypt for mistreating His firstborn son, Israel. The powerful Egyptian empire fell, as God prophesied, and never again emerged as a significant world power.

The same is true for many nations that have mistreated the Jews over the centuries. Most of them are shells of their former glory, and some no longer even exist as a people group.

Whenever I enter a church that has closed its heart to reaching the Jews, I can sense, even before the pastor has preached a word, that they are not walking in the fullness of God's blessing. But churches that show their love for the Jews and Israel by taking the gospel to them have an extra measure of the anointing and liberty. It's not that God doesn't love or bless other churches. But His Word clearly states, "I will bless those who bless you, and I will curse him who curses you" (Genesis 12:3).

This is an unchangeable principle in the Word of God concerning how God will bless us (or not) based on how we treat the descendants of Abraham, the Jews. The greatest way we can bless the Jews is by bringing their gospel back to them (Acts 3:26). We limit the measure of God's blessing when we ignore His heart for reaching His people.

How Can a Nation Be God's Firstborn?

The firstborn opens the womb of the mother, and Israel opened the "womb" of God. God first revealed himself to mankind through the Jews.

When God called Abraham, people were worshipping many deities. The knowledge of the one true God had been all but lost due to the fall in the garden of Eden. But once again God chose to reveal himself to mankind, this time through Abraham, by calling him out of an idolatrous nation and starting a new nation through his seed. Figuratively, God's spiritual womb was opened on the earth through Israel so He could have a people for himself, who would manifest His glory on the earth.

As a result, the one true God became forever known as the God of Israel. He said that they were called to be "a kingdom of priests and a holy nation" (Exodus 19:6).

What we now know as monotheism was introduced to the world through the Jewish nation. Throughout the Old Testament we see how the one true God revealed himself to the nations that worshipped idols and false gods, and thus His name and His fame spread throughout the earth.

Through the tribe of Judah, Israel brought forth the only begotten Son of God to redeem mankind. Jesus is referred to as "the firstborn from the dead" (Revelation 1:5).

In addition, He was the firstborn son of His earthly mother, so He was "holy to the Lord" from birth by reason of opening His mother's womb. Luke 2:22–24 says:

> When the days of her purification according to the law of Moses
> were completed, they [Joseph and Mary] brought Him to Jerusalem
> to present Him to the Lord (as it is written in the law of the Lord,

"Every male who opens the womb shall be called holy to the Lord"), and to offer a sacrifice according to what is said in the law of the Lord, "A pair of turtledoves or two young pigeons."

Of course, Jesus was already holy because He was without sin from the beginning. But Jesus also opened the womb of His mother, making Him "holy to the Lord" in that way as well. Israel is still holy to God. Even though their actions are not always holy, they are still His chosen people in that they are set apart for His purposes. He has not rejected Israel for her sins, just as He has not rejected us for our sins. So let us take the gospel once again to God's firstborn and let them know that their Messiah has come!

REASON #7. ISRAEL IS THE FIRSTFRUITS OF GOD'S HARVEST

Scripture teaches that tithing is one of the keys to financial prosperity. Giving God the firstfruits of our income (the first 10 percent) doesn't make sense in the natural. But with God, less (with His blessing on it) goes further than more without His blessing.

That really is how it works in the kingdom. When we give the first 10 percent of our financial resources to God, we activate the supernatural. If I have a thousand dollars and I don't tithe on it, it will actually deplete more quickly than if I tithe a hundred dollars and have only nine hundred left to spend. I have tithed throughout my whole life as a believer and can attest to this truth.

Even when I couldn't make ends meet on paper, I still tithed. It's our way of acknowledging that provision for our needs is not our responsibility but God's. It shows we trust in His supernatural provision instead of in the work of our hands. I would rather have nine hundred dollars blessed by God than one thousand dollars all to myself.

The tithe is "holy to the Lord" (Leviticus 27:30), which means it belongs to Him. This is why we bring the tithe to God. We don't really give it, because it already belongs to Him.

In the same way, we are called to tithe spiritually into the
Great Commission by bringing the gospel to the firstfruits of
God's harvest, the Jews. We see this demonstrated in Jeremiah 2:3,
which says, "Israel was holy to the Lord" (NIV). This does not mean
that Israel was perfect. It means that Israel belongs to God. When
something is called "holy to the Lord," that means it belongs to Him
or is set apart to Him.

This verse goes on to say Israel was "the firstfruits of his harvest"
(NIV). Jesus referred to the mission field as a harvest in Luke 10:1–2,
when he sent out the seventy-two disciples. He said, "The harvest
is plentiful, but the workers are few. Ask the Lord of the harvest,
therefore, to send out workers into his harvest field" (NIV). Jesus was
sending the disciples out to preach the gospel and to win souls for the
kingdom, using a farming term that his listeners could relate to.

Israel has always been God's pride and joy, just as any father feels
about his firstborn son. I have three wonderful sons and of course I
love them all equally. But the one who opened his mother's womb
has a special place in my heart. If anyone ever messed with him, that
person would have to deal with my wrath.

In the same way, God is protective of the firstfruits of his harvest,
Israel. Jeremiah 2:3 (NIV) goes on to say, "All who devoured her were
held guilty, and disaster overtook them." Scripture warns repeatedly
that God will judge any nation or individual who comes against the
Jewish people.

The New King James Version of Jeremiah 2:3 says that Israel
was "the firstfruits of his increase" (emphasis added). This word is a
financial term, often used in conjunction with tithing or giving an
offering to God.

If we tithe spiritually by taking the gospel to the Jew first, God
will supernaturally bless and increase the rest of the harvest. We see
this demonstrated in the book of Acts as Paul and Barnabas followed
this pattern, which we are to emulate.

Taking the gospel to the Jewish people is not a burden but a
joyful, incredible privilege. As we share the gospel with the lost
sheep of the house of Israel, God will back us up with his love, his
wisdom, and an unlimited outpouring of his Holy Spirit. Obeying
his commands is never burdensome. As Jesus says in Matthew 11:30,
"My yoke is easy and My burden is light." When we take up his yoke,

we will find rest for our souls. Others will find rest for their souls, too, as they hear the good news through us.

At Gateway Church, where Robert Morris is the senior pastor, they have tithed into the Jewish harvest as their firstfruits, giving to Jewish missions every month since their conception. Fifteen percent of Gateway's total budget goes to missions and is stewarded well by the Global Department, of which I was a part. The first 10 percent of that 15 percent goes to ministries in Israel and around the world that are effectively reaching Jewish people with the gospel.

We believe that this is one of the reasons Gateway has been so supernaturally blessed. After only thirteen years as a church, we have a budget exceeding fifty million dollars, and we sometimes have as many as thirty thousand people in attendance on a single weekend. During the recent recession, when people were being laid off work in droves and many churches around the country had to close their doors because of the financial strain this put on them, Gateway successfully embarked on our largest building program to date. They built a state-of-the-art, four-thousand-seat auditorium to accommodate our growth. I have no doubt that this was God's way of saying to the leadership, "You have been faithful and obedient to reach out to my kids (the Jews) with the gospel. Now I will take care of your kids." Gateway Church continues to grow and prosper, financially and numerically, as well as in depth and love among its members.

Because they believe that the gospel is to the Jew first, they hold a "firstfruits service" on the first Friday of every month. This messianic Jewish service has almost all of the elements you'd find in a synagogue service, including a handwritten (kosher) Torah from Israel. The main difference is that Yeshua is presented as the promised Messiah. He is the focus and fulcrum of these services. God blesses these services greatly with his presence and with many seekers.

In my thirty years of ministry to Jewish people, most of the messianic services I've attended around the US average about a hundred attendees. But during these twelve services a year at Gateway, when I was leading them we averaged around five hundred in attendance, and during the Jewish festivals we often

had well over a thousand. Jewish seekers regularly gave their
hearts to the Lord at these services.

We were also reaching the Christian community with an
understanding of and appreciation for the roots of their faith.

REASON #8. IT IS GOD'S PASSION.

In Romans 10:1 Paul reveals God's greatest desire for Israel.
"Brethren, my heart's desire and prayer to God for Israel is that
they may be saved." There is no other way for a Jewish person to
be saved except through the Jewish Messiah, Jesus.

Many evangelical Christians are now standing with Israel and
the Jewish people. Today's attitude sure beats the anti-Semitism
we have seen in the past, and I fully support this. However, almost
every evangelical church, movement, ministry, and organization
stops short of God's primary goal for the Jewish people, which
is their salvation. In fact, some Christian groups actually resist
preaching the gospel to the Jews.

I am grateful to the recent pro-Israel evangelical movement.
However, the focus of this movement is usually to stand with
Israel morally and politically. While this is a good thing in itself, it
should not be to the exclusion of bringing the gospel to the Jewish
people. Evangelism to the Jews is not emphasized, most likely for
fear of offending or upsetting the Jewish community.

As a Jew who believes in the Messiah, I find this strange,
because Jesus is more central and relevant to Jewish culture, both
historically and eternally, than any individual will ever be. Why
would anyone want to deny the Jewish people the only lasting
hope for their nation and for them as individuals?

It seems that there is an unspoken polarization in Christian
circles that support Israel, where either you stand with Israel
as a nation or you share the gospel with the Jews, as if the two
contradict each other. But in reality, we are called to do both,
according to the Scriptures.

In Romans 9:1–5 we have one of the deepest insights in all
Scripture into the heart of Jesus. Through the writings of Paul,
inspired by the Holy Spirit, we see the passion of God for his
chosen people and the lengths to which he is willing to go to

reach them. Paul's opening statement in verse 1 is: "I tell the truth in Christ, I am not lying, my conscience also bearing me witness in the Holy Spirit." Paul obviously feels very strongly about what he is about to say. He wants us to see the depth of his sincerity on this matter and its importance to him and to God. First he says, "I tell the truth in Christ," to firmly establish his point. He goes on to say, "I am not lying," as if trying to convince anyone who might doubt his sincerity. Next he brings his human spirit and God's Spirit into the picture, saying, "… my conscience also bearing me witness in the Holy Spirit." Paul must be building up to something of immense importance to God's heart to have prefaced it in so many ways before making his point.

In verse 2, he says, "I have great sorrow and continual grief in my heart." The Holy Spirit has placed on Paul's heart the message he is about to give so strongly that Paul has great sorrow and continual grief.

What can this be that is so heavy on God's heart? Paul explains in verse 3. "I would pray that I myself were cursed, banished from Messiah for the sake of my people—my own flesh and blood" (TLV). Paul's burden for the salvation of his countrymen, the Jews, was so great that he was willing to be accursed if that would bring about their salvation.

The Greek word used here for "cursed" is *anathema*. This word means to be permanently cut off from God and separated from him forever. Paul is saying that he would be willing to go to hell for all eternity if that would result in the salvation of his Jewish brethren.

Now, I am a very loyal friend. I have stood up for my friends even at the risk of my own physical well-being. But I am not willing to go to hell for anyone, not even for a second. For one thing, I would be too afraid I wouldn't be able to get out. But more important, I could not bear to go to any place where I am cut off from the presence of God, even temporarily. Yet Paul was willing to be permanently shut out of the presence of God and to remain in hell forever if that would result in the salvation of his Jewish brethren.

The Jewish people must hold a strategic place in God's heart and his eternal plan for mankind for the Holy Spirit to have moved Paul's heart for them to such a great extent.

In verse 4, Paul gives us a clue as to why reaching the Jews with the gospel is so close to God's heart. He says, "... Israelites, to whom pertain the adoption, the glory, the covenants, the giving of the law, the service of God, and the promises." All of the covenants we enjoy the blessings of today—the biblical promises we base our lives on, the giving of the Law (on which the judicial systems of most nations are based, whether they acknowledge it or not), the glory of God that we experience today in worship—all came to us through the Jewish people.

Paul goes on to say in verse 5, "To them belong the patriarchs—and from them, according to the flesh, the Messiah, who is over all, God, blessed forever. Amen" (TLV). The biblical fathers of the faith (Abraham, Isaac, and Jacob) and those who came after them were all Jews. Paul climaxes his exhortation by saying that even Jesus himself, according to his natural human lineage, came into the world as a Jew.

The Jews still play a crucial role in God's plan. And reaching them with the gospel plays a major role in God's purpose for the human race. Paul had such a burning passion to reach his Jewish brethren with the gospel that he was even willing to go to hell for them. This leads me to one question: are we even willing to preach the gospel to them? Or is their eternal salvation not important enough to us to possibly endure a few moments of discomfort for fear of rejection?

REASON #9. ISRAEL'S SALVATION IS A MAJOR KEY TO WORLDWIDE REVIVAL.

In Romans 11:11–15, Paul speaks about the role of the Jewish people in relation to the gospel and God's plan for mankind as a whole. He starts off with a rhetorical question: "Have they [the Jews] stumbled that they should fall?" In other words, have they stumbled beyond recovery? He immediately and emphatically answers his own question with a resounding rebuttal. "Certainly not!" He goes on to explain, "But through their fall, to provoke them to jealousy, salvation has come to the Gentiles." As a result of the Jews' rejection of Jesus on a national level, salvation was made available to the Gentile nations.

Paul says in verse 12, "Now if their fall is riches for the world, and their failure riches for the Gentiles, how much more their fullness!" If the Jewish rejection of Jesus meant spiritual riches and salvation for the Gentiles, can you imagine what will happen to the Gentile world when the Jews accept Jesus?

Paul addressed his Gentile readers in verse 13, saying that he hoped his ministry to them would "provoke to jealousy those who are my flesh and save some of them" (v. 14). Even Paul, the greatest apostle to the Gentiles who ever lived, was thinking of how he could use his calling to the Gentiles to ultimately reach the Jews.

The English word *jealousy* is not the best translation of the original Greek here. That word denotes a frustrated and negative state. The King James Version has a more accurate translation. It says to "provoke to emulation." Paul's desire was that when Jews saw Gentiles worshipping and experiencing a living and dynamic relationship with the God of Israel, they would want to have that for themselves.

I have seen this happen in my own life. When I was working as a volunteer at a kibbutz in Israel, on the beautiful coastline outside Tel Aviv, I shared a room with two other guys. One was a friend I was traveling with. When the other guy moved out, the one who moved in was a born-again Christian. I didn't even know what that meant. But I noticed that Frank loved the Jewish people, and he seemed to have a personal relationship with God. There was an assurance about him, a sense of certainty and purpose, as if he knew where he was from and where he was going in life. I appeared to have that confidence on the outside, due to my popularity with the girls, my reputation as a fighter, and my macho bravado. But inside I felt lost, in need of direction.

How could this Gentile have a relationship with the God of Israel that I, a Jew, did not? That gave me a lot of food for thought. Frank provoked in me a desire to emulate him, but I didn't know how to get there.

Because I felt I could never have that kind of faith, I played devil's advocate whenever he tried to share his beliefs. I always gave him a hard time, making out with my girlfriend and drinking in front of him, and asking him to join our parties, just to irritate him. Even though he had what I wanted, I never let him know. Still, he played a major role in my salvation, even though I didn't realize it at the time.

Verse 15 brings us to the climax point of this message. Paul says, "If their being cast away is the reconciling of the world, what will their acceptance be but life from the dead?" The punctuation here implies that Paul is asking a question. But he is actually making an exclamation. The Good News Translation brings out the intended meaning much better. It says, "When they were rejected, all other people were changed from God's enemies into his friends. What will it be, then, when they are accepted? It will be life for the dead!"

Paul is saying that the Jewish rejection of Jesus brought salvation to mankind, and their acceptance of him will bring life from the dead. And isn't that the very definition of revival?

The salvation of the Jewish people is going to usher in the greatest worldwide spiritual awakening mankind has ever known. We are already seeing the beginnings of this revival. Before Jerusalem came back into Jewish hands in 1967, there were only a handful of Jewish believers around the world. Since that time, more Jews have been swept into the kingdom than we have seen since the first century, when the church was birthed through the Jewish believers in Jerusalem at Pentecost. Prior to 1967, almost all of the churches in Israel were international church plants. Today there are more than 120 indigenous messianic Jewish congregations in Israel, and thousands of Jews are coming to a belief in Jesus all around the world.

I do not believe this is a coincidence. Since 1967 the church has experienced the greatest worldwide revival in history. Millions have been ushered into the kingdom.

Jesus spoke clearly about the fulfillment of the "times of the Gentiles" in Luke 21:24. "They will fall by the edge of the sword, and be led away captive into all nations. And Jerusalem will be trampled by Gentiles until the times of the Gentiles are fulfilled."

Jerusalem is the eternal Jewish capital. The Gentile occupation of the holy city came to an end during the Six-Day War of 1967, thus fulfilling Jesus' prophecy that Jerusalem would be restored to the Jews. This initiated the restoration of the kingdom to the Jewish people and indicated the fulfillment of the "times of the Gentiles." Of course, this does not mean that God has stopped saving Gentiles. Rather, it indicates that the Jews and Israel will once again play a major role in advancing the kingdom of God on the earth.

Paul alluded to this in Romans 11:25, saying that a "blindness in part" would happen to Israel "until the fullness of the Gentiles has come in." This event is the turning point for the spiritual restoration of Israel.

Shortly after his resurrection, the disciples asked Jesus, "Lord, will You at this time restore the kingdom to Israel?" (Acts 1:6). He replied, "It is not for you to know times or seasons which the Father has put in His own authority" (v. 7).

Almost two thousand years after that question was asked, we are finally living in those times. Before our very eyes, we are seeing the kingdom of God being restored to Israel. How the early disciples longed to see the days we are now living in!

In the early '70s, many Jews were brought into the kingdom during what was known as the Jesus movement. Many of those Jewish believers are now leaders in the messianic movement.

A worldwide revival, in connection with the restoration of Israel and the Jews, was predicted by the apostle Paul and the ancient Hebrew prophets. It was also foreseen by some of the greatest church fathers in centuries past.

In *A Puritan Golden Treasury*, John Owen, perhaps the most renowned of all the Puritan theologians in the 1600s, is quoted as saying, "There is not any promise anywhere of raising up a kingdom unto the Lord Jesus Christ in this world but it is either expressed, or clearly intimated, that at the beginning it must be with the Jews."[1]

Robert Leighton, a contemporary of Owen, wrote:

---

[1] I. D. E. Thomas, *A Puritan Golden Treasury* (Carlisle, PA: Banner of Truth Trust, 1977), 155.

They forget a main point for the Church's glory, who pray not daily for the conversion [turning] of the Jews. ... Undoubtedly, that the people of the Jews shall once more be commanded to arise and shine, and their return shall be the riches of the Gentiles (Romans 11:12), and that shall be a more glorious time than ever the Church of God did yet behold.[2]

About thirty years ago, it was extremely rare to meet a Jewish believer. Today, there are an estimated 300,000 messianic Jews worldwide.[3] There are almost twenty thousand Jewish believers and about 150 congregations in Israel alone.[4] This is a foretaste of the worldwide spiritual awakening predicted in the Bible.

Jews are coming to the Lord all around the world, in Israel and in other nations. God is moving among the Jews in the US, the former Soviet Union, South Africa, Mexico, Argentina, Canada, Ethiopia, Zimbabwe, and every other nation where Jews dwell. This is the firstfruits of a great revival among the Jewish people.

Corresponding to this Jewish restoration, we are seeing a worldwide move of God in which millions are being birthed into the kingdom all over the world. This is happening in Asian countries as well as all around the African continent and even eastern Europe, where there has been an explosion of large churches. Many of these churches are sending missionaries to unreached countries, where the gospel is being secretly preached through underground churches and cell groups.

God is also moving among the Muslims. Even in countries where Islam is the predominant religion and the gospel is forbidden, people are seeing visions of Jesus and coming to faith. I was ministering in Ashdod, Israel, recently, and an Iranian Jewish woman came up to me and told me she'd had a vision of a man in white robes. He appeared by her bed when her room was dark and told her he was the Messiah. I explained to her that the man in her vision was Yeshua, the promised Messiah of Israel. She began

---

[2]Ibid., 156– 157.
[3]Troy Anderson, "Where Your Israel Donation Really Goes," Charisma Magazine, October 2013.
[4]Ibid.

to weep and gave her heart to Jesus. Later that night, her daughter accepted Jesus as well.

We are experiencing the biggest worldwide spiritual awakening our planet has ever seen. And this global revival has only just begun!

TITHING INTO THE GREAT COMMISSION

Romans 11:16 says, "If the first piece of bread is given to God, then the whole loaf is his also" (GNT). If we make the Jews the firstfruits of our outreach, God will bless and multiply our efforts, and we will bring in a huge Gentile harvest too. This verse goes on to say, "If the roots of a tree (the Jews) are offered to God, the branches (the Gentiles) are his also" (GNT).

We see this same principle demonstrated in the prophecies of the Old Testament. Zechariah 8:22–23 says:

> Many peoples and strong nations shall come to seek the Lord of hosts in Jerusalem, and to pray before the Lord. Thus says the Lord of hosts: "In those days ten men from every language of the nations shall grasp the sleeve of a Jewish man, saying, 'Let us go with you, for we have heard that God is with you.'"

In the end times the Jews will be used mightily to bring the Gentile nations back to God. We don't know exactly how or when God will bring this amazing prophecy to pass, but we know that he will.

Approximately seven thousand languages exist in the world.[5] If ten Gentiles from every language came to know God through a Jew, as this prophecy of Zechariah implies, that would total almost seventy thousand people coming to know the Lord through each Jewish believer.

If we can reach the Jews successfully, we will in turn reach the whole world. That is another key reason to follow God's pattern of bringing the gospel to the Jew first and then to the Gentile. By doing this we are tithing spiritually into the Great Commission,

---

[5] *Ethnologue*, the most extensive catalog of the world's languages, published by SIL International, recorded 6,909 languages in 2009.

which will activate a greater anointing on the rest of our outreach efforts in the same way that tithing on our income activates a greater blessing and increase on our finances.

PART TWO

HINDRANCES TO FULFILLING GOD'S BLUEPRINT

Ever since God called Abraham and promised great things for him and his descendants, the Devil has been intent on destroying the Jewish people. Satan knows he can't destroy God or even touch Him, so he goes for the thing closest to God, which is His people. This is why Jews and born-again Christians are coming under increased attack in today's world.

These people groups have more in common than just a monotheistic religion because even the Muslims claim to have this. They both worship the one true God of the Bible, the God of Abraham, Isaac, and Jacob. No Christian would say that he worships a different God from the Jews. Yet many act as if there are two Gods: the Gentile version, who is over the church, and the Jewish version, who is the God of Israel. Many Gentile Christians have unintentionally extracted themselves from their Jewish roots and the Jewish version of Jesus. But there is only one God, and He is the God of Israel.

On the one hand, Gentiles don't need to be "Judaized." But on the other hand, we don't want to "Gentilize" God, either. Let us worship Him for who He is, the God of Israel. Since God chose to forever link His name to the first three Jews in history, Christians should never be ashamed of their Jewish brethren or the Jewish roots of their faith.

In fact, anyone who calls himself a Christian should, by nature, have a deep love and loyalty, as well as a voluntary sense of indebtedness, toward the Jewish people. God chose to bring salvation to the world through a Jewish person: Jesus. Through the Jews came the very "oracles of God" (Romans 3:2).

There should naturally be an unbreakable, unshakeable bond between these two people groups who, alone in this dark and needy world, stand for the one true God, the only hope of the human race. Yet, sadly, this has not been so. Over the last two thousand years, the relationship between Christians and Jews has been fraught with distrust, betrayal, and demonization. The Enemy has successfully lodged a tremendous wedge between these two groups.

There are numerous hindrances to fulfilling God's blueprint of taking the gospel to the Jew first. In this section, I will identify the top ten obstacles I have come across in my ministry. The first two are related to church history; the next eight are related to false doctrines and misguided belief systems.

HINDRANCE #1. CHRISTIAN ANTI-SEMITISM

When Jewish people think of the Christian church—particularly in my generation, whose ancestors came directly from Europe—we think of the Holocaust, the Spanish Inquisition, the Crusades. Growing up, I thought that church was where Christians gathered to discuss how evil the Jews were for killing Christ.

You might think that idea sounds far-fetched or paranoid, but my grandparents experienced this firsthand in the early twentieth century. Orthodox Catholic and Russian priests in Eastern Europe often preached fiery sermons against the Jews, especially on Easter, accusing them of deicide (killing God). They even spread rumors of what they called "blood libel," claiming that Jews killed Christian children and used their blood to make matzo (unleavened bread) for Passover. As ridiculous as this sounds to us, many of the ignorant masses believed these lies, and terrible pogroms against the Jews ensued as a result.

In my grandparents' day, Russian Cossacks regularly invaded Jewish villages on horseback, a priest with a giant cross at the helm, and destroyed their property, raped the women, and beat up the men, often maiming or killing them in the process. Many of my relatives had to flee Eastern Europe for their lives. Thousands of Jews ended up in South Africa. Many others found refuge in the US, Canada, Argentina, and Australia.

This turned out to be God's hand of preservation and mercy, because a much worse attack was about to happen that would make the pogroms look tame in comparison. In the Holocaust of WW2, six million Jewish people were killed in an attempt to rid the world of Jews once and for all. If not for the pogroms of Eastern Europe, which drove the Jews to find refuge in civilized nations, Hitler might have wiped out the entire Jewish population.

My grandparents witnessed multiple violent attacks on Jewish people and their property by the Cossacks and the Orthodox Christian community. In the early twentieth century, they found refuge in South Africa, along with thousands of other Lithuanian Jews. Those Jews who decided to remain were not so fortunate. In 1941, the Nazis took all the people in the Jewish community in my grandmother's village out of their homes, forced them to march into the forest, made them strip naked, and massacred them there. Only one rabbi survived from that village to tell the story.

In the village my grandfather came from, about fifteen miles away, all the men, women, and children were herded into a building in the village square, and the Nazis set it on fire. They all suffocated or burned to death.

Of course, the Holocaust was perpetrated by Nazis, not Christians (at least by biblical definition). But almost all Germans were members of the Catholic church, the Lutheran state church, or some other Protestant denomination. In the concentration camps, guards played "Silent Night" over loudspeakers at Christmas. So in the eyes of the Jews, the Nazis were Christians.

Unfortunately, a similar attitude is still prevalent today. Christians sometimes quote New Testament passages as justification for their prejudices. Even though they are taking these quotes out of context, this prevents Jews from reading the New Testament the way they do the Old Testament, because they are afraid it is full of hatred for them and their people. Many Jewish children (myself included) have been forbidden from reading the New Testament because their families were taught it is an anti-Semitic book.

HINDRANCE #2. MARTIN LUTHER'S TEACHINGS

Martin Luther accomplished many positive things in his lifetime. He brought about the Reformation and the birthing of what we know today as the Protestant church, in all its various forms and denominations. He brought to light the truth of salvation by grace through faith alone (Ephesians 2:8–10) at a time when the Catholic church had suppressed the masses and kept them in bondage and darkness, trying to earn their salvation through various forms of penance and good works and loyalty to the Catholic church. Luther played a major role in encouraging the average man to read the Bible for himself instead of blindly believing everything the priests told him. He was a biblical scholar and renowned theologian who translated the Bible into an easy-to-read version in the contemporary German language of his time. The Luther Bible contributed hugely to the Reformation movement that we enjoy the fruit of to this day, giving the common man access to the Scriptures in language he could read for himself.

However, Martin Luther had an extremely anti-Semitic side that we rarely talk about. Some of his rantings against the Jews, and his solution to the "Jewish problem" of his day, sound an awful lot like Hitler. And many of Hitler's statements and actions reflect Martin Luther's writings. I believe that these teachings played a significant role in preparing the German people to allow the Holocaust to happen in their nation.

In 1543, Luther published a book called *The Jews and their Lies*. In it he advised the German leadership of his day concerning what they should do about the "Jewish problem" in their midst.[6] This book set the stage for Hitler to put these abominations into practice when he came to power about four hundred years later.

Below are seven of the things Luther recommended in this book that Hitler put into practice, in many cases word for word.[7]

1. The synagogues should be set on fire.

    On November 9, 1938, many synagogues in Germany were set on fire in the infamous event now known as Kristallnacht ("night of the broken glass"). As these buildings burned, Jews were beaten and brutalized, and more than ninety killed, while the local citizens and police stood idly by. This event played a major role in the desensitization of the German people to public mistreatment and even murder of Jews, thus preparing them to be silent to the mass killings in concentration camps.

2. Jews should not be allowed to own houses; instead they should be placed in a stable like Gypsies.

    Hitler ordered his Nazis to drive Jews out of their homes, stating that they were not allowed to own "German" property. Then he put them into mass ghettos and allowed Germans to occupy their homes.

---

[6]Michael L. Brown, Our Hands Are Stained with Blood: The Tragic Story of the "Church" and the Jewish People (Shippensburg, PA: Destiny Image Publishers, 1992), 14– 15.

[7]Frank Ephraim Talmage, ed., Disputation and Dialogue: Readings in the Jewish- Christian Encounter (New York: KTAV/Anti- Defamation League of B'nai B'rith, 1975), 34– 40.

3. All Jewish prayer books and Talmuds should be taken away since they teach lying, cursing, and blaspheming.

   The Nazis publicly burned huge piles of Jewish prayer books and Torah scrolls outside the synagogues.

4. Rabbis should be prohibited from teaching under threat of losing body and soul.

   Hitler's SS beat many rabbis to death outside or near their synagogues, plucked out their beards and set them on fire, and did other things too horrible to mention.

5. Protection of Jews on highways should be revoked so they will stay at home.

   Hitler had Jews' passports revoked, along with their German citizenship. Then he made all Jewish people wear a yellow Star of David to identify them as Jews. If they were seen in public, Germans could spit on them and beat them without consequence. Jews were denied traveling privileges, and curfews were imposed at night, forcing them to stay in their homes or risk being severely beaten or shot.

6. Jewish usury (money lending) should be prohibited.

   Hitler took this to the next level, refusing to allow Jews to have their own businesses. Even before their businesses were closed down completely, Jews were forbidden to sell to non-Jews.

7. Young, strong Jews should be forced to earn their bread by the sweat of their brows, flailing axes and spindles.

   Hitler conscripted young, strong Jews into forced labor, promising those who entered the concentration camps that hard work would bring freedom. As they entered the camps, they passed under signs with the now infamous words *Arbeit Macht Frei,* meaning "Work makes (you) free." This, of course, was a lie. Many of those who were not immediately sent to the gas chambers eventually became so weakened from starvation and disease that they could hardly work. Once they were no longer considered to be of any use to the Germans, they were shot or gassed.

8. Luther concluded his list of recommendations with the most chilling one of all. "To sum up, dear princes and nobles who have Jews in your domains, if this advice of mine does not suit you, then find a better one so that you and we may all be free of this insufferable devilish burden called the Jews."

In Hitler's time, when a village or town was completely purged of Jews because they had all been exterminated or deported to concentration camps, the Nazis would put up a huge banner, often outside a synagogue, declaring it *Judenfrai* ("Jew free"). This disturbing declaration certainly indicates that Hitler took to heart (sometimes to the letter) Martin Luther's recommendation to find a solution to "this insufferable devilish burden called the Jews."

While Martin Luther was not solely responsible for searing the national German conscience, his anti-Semitic writings certainly played a major role to this end. His book was used as a propaganda tool to demonize and vilify the Jews, and in Nazi rallies leading up to the Holocaust.

A good friend of mine named Craig Beling, who is an international lawyer and graduated from Harvard with honors, told me that on a purely legal basis, if Martin Luther were taken to court in a modern American trial, the implementation of any one of his suggestions would constitute a felony under United States law. If death resulted from any of these activities, he would be subject to the possibility of life imprisonment or the death penalty.

In today's society, Martin Luther would be considered a dangerous extremist who should be watched closely by the Department of Homeland Security, not a hero and the founder of an entire Christian denomination.

Luther's anti-Semitic rantings also became a major stumbling block to bringing the gospel to the Jews. After all, why would they want to worship the Christian God, whom Martin Luther claimed despised them for supposedly killing His Son, especially when Luther accused them of being murderers of Christian children and a "devilish burden" to German society?

I am not saying we should refuse to honor Martin Luther for his contribution to the Reformation. But I feel strongly that when he is mentioned from the pulpit for his contribution to church history, his name should always be mentioned with a disclaimer, to be fair to both Christians and Jews.

Second Corinthians 6:3 (NIV) says, "We put no stumbling block in anyone's path, so that our ministry will not be discredited." Martin Luther's teachings concerning the Jews have been a huge hindrance to the cause of Jewish evangelism. He is honored as one of the greatest church leaders in history, yet his teachings paved the way for Hitler to justify the Holocaust. To most Christians he is seen as a hero. But to the Jewish world he represents the worst of what Christianity came to represent in terms of anti-Semitism over the last two millennia.

Even including a statement like "Luther's teachings regarding the Jewish people do not represent God's heart or the Scriptures" would be a step in the right direction. A small step, to be sure. But God can take small things, like fishes and loaves, and feed thousands. He can use our small but humble words to begin a big healing in Jewish hearts, so they can see their Messiah and be saved.

Despite the horrors of the Holocaust, God's plans for the Jews have not been thwarted. They cannot be, because, as the Scriptures say in Jeremiah 31:35–36 (NIV):

> This is what the LORD says, he who appoints the sun to shine by day, who decrees the moon and stars to shine by night, who stirs up the sea so that its waves roar—the LORD Almighty is his name: "Only if these decrees vanish from my sight," declares the LORD, "will Israel ever cease being a nation before me."

Whenever I see the sun shining during the day, and the stars and moon at night, I am reminded that God still has a plan for my people. What an immeasurably great promise!

HINDRANCE #3. VILIFICATION OF ISRAEL

God, in his sovereignty, foresaw the impending disaster of the Holocaust and put a plan in place beforehand to save a people for himself. Out of the ashes and horrors, a nation was born in one day (as prophesied in Isaiah 66:8). In May of 1948, Israel was voted a nation by the UN Assembly. Once again the Jewish people could hold their heads high, as they now had their own nation and their own defense force.

And yet, Israel had no rest from her enemies. The hostile Arab countries around her attacked almost immediately after she declared her independence, vowing to "drive the Jews into the sea."[8] Since then, God has miraculously preserved Israel through five major wars and many Arab uprisings.

Even today, Christians are attacking Israel in their own way. For example, the Presbyterian General Assembly recently voted in favor of boycotting goods made in settlements in Israel, and narrowly voted against divesting holdings in three multinational companies that do business in those settlements.[9]

I wonder if these voters realized they were hurting the brothers of Jesus, whom they claim to serve and believe in. Maybe they forgot that Jesus was a Jew, and if He lived on earth today, Israel would be His home country. How can Christians boycott Jesus' nation and His people? This anti-Israel stance is the result of the church departing from her biblical Jewish roots.

---

[8]Jonathan S. Tobin, "Jews Driven into the Sea at Last," Commentary magazine, May 7, 2009 (www.commentarymagazine.com/2009/05/07/jews-driven-into-the-sea-at-last/).

[9]Natasha Mozgovaya, "Presbyterian Church in U.S. Votes to Boycott Israeli Settlement Goods," Haaretz magazine, July 6, 2012 (http://www.haaretz.com/news/diplomacy-defense/presbyterian-church-in-us-votes-to-boycott-israeli- settlement-goods-1.449329)

Despite all this opposition, Israel is again becoming established, both in numbers and in influence. Jewish communities around the world are once again thriving and becoming strong culturally, economically, and socially in this post-Holocaust era.

The Enemy's plan now is more subtle and sinister than torture, genocide, and war, because it is not visible to the naked eye. The Devil has come to terms with the fact that he can never destroy the Jewish people physically, so his new tactic is to destroy them spiritually. He is now trying to bring about a "spiritual holocaust" by keeping the light of the gospel from the Jews. The most effective way for him to do this is by preventing Christians from sharing the good news with their Jewish brethren. His tactics range from blatant false doctrines to casual indifference to ignorance of God's plan for the Jews.

The following hindrances are false doctrines or wrong belief systems that have nearly brought Jewish evangelism to a standstill among many Christians today.

HINDRANCE #4. REPLACEMENT THEOLOGY

This theology teaches that the church has replaced Israel in God's plan of salvation and that He is now finished with the Jewish people as a nation. It claims that God has rejected Israel for rejecting Jesus as their Messiah, and all the promises that He gave to the Jewish people are now void. They have been transferred to the church, the "new Israel" or "spiritual Israel."

Here are the reasons this doctrine is false and so destructive in fulfilling God's blueprint for the Great Commission:

• It has no biblical foundation or precedent.

Jeremiah 31:31–34 clearly describes what the new covenant is and whom God made it with. Verse 31 says, "'The days are coming,' says the Lord, 'when I will make a new covenant with the house of Israel and with the house of Judah.'"

About seven hundred years before Jesus was born, Jeremiah looked into the future and prophetically described the new covenant that was to come. The first thing he said was that it would be with the house of Israel and the house of Judah. At that time, Israel was divided into the northern and southern kingdoms: the house of Israel in the north and the house of Judah in the south. The Scripture passage here is referring to the whole Jewish nation.

When people today hear the phrase *old covenant,* the images that come to mind are usually distinctively Jewish. They think of Moses with the Israelites in the desert, the parting of the Red Sea, the giving of the Law, animal sacrifices, the temple, etc. But when someone mentions the new covenant, people usually associate that with distinctly Christian images. A church building with a cross on the roof, perhaps. Or maybe a stained-glass image of Jesus in which He has a lamb on His shoulders and a gold halo around His head. They might think of lyrics from a Christian hymn, Jesus surrounded by His disciples, or an empty cross.

Or someone might think of the famous Christian painting by Leonardo da Vinci that allegedly depicts Jesus and His disciples at the Last Supper. In truth, this scene looks more like European choir boys partaking in a stiff formal dinner than a gathering of hardy men from the Middle East celebrating the Passover. Even though all the men at the Last Supper were Jews, the only one in this portrayal who looks even remotely Jewish is Judas, the betrayer—and he resembles a Jewish caricature. This painting is typical of the art of that era, which vilified Jews and elevated Christians.

Most people do not automatically associate the phrase *new covenant* with the Jewish people. But according to the Scriptures, the new covenant was made with the Jewish nation, just like the old covenant was.

To the early believers, the new covenant was so clearly made between God and the Jewish people that it took two supernatural acts of God (Peter's vision on his roof and a direct revelation to Paul) to persuade them that it was for Gentiles as well and not exclusively for Jews.

At that time, Gentiles were not allowed anywhere near the inner courts of the temple, and certainly not into the Holy of Holies. So the Jews presumed they would also be excluded from his holy presence under the new covenant. But God gave the apostle Paul a revelation about the Gentiles in Ephesians 2:11–14a (TLV):

> Therefore, keep in mind that once you—Gentiles in the flesh—were called "uncircumcision" by those called "circumcision" (which is performed on flesh by hand). At that time you were separate from Messiah, excluded from the commonwealth of Israel and strangers to the covenants of promise, having no hope and without God in the world. But now in Messiah *Yeshua*, you who once were far off [referring to Gentiles] have been brought near by the blood of Messiah. For he is our shalom [peace], the One who made the two into one and broke down the middle wall of separation.

The new covenant was originally made with Israel. But when Isaiah prophesied that those walking in darkness would one day see a great light (9:1–2), he was foreseeing the time when the gospel would also be preached to the Gentiles, so they too would have access to God. This first happened when Peter brought the gospel to Cornelius and his household. Later Paul brought it to the rest of the Gentile world.

Jeremiah's prophecy shatters the myth of Replacement Theology. For Christians today to say that God has replaced Israel with the church shows how far we have strayed from the Bible in many modern seminaries.

• God is a God of covenant.

Some proponents of Replacement Theology say that God has rejected Israel because of their sins and disobedience over the centuries. But the church is guilty of the same sins they have accused the Jews of over the centuries, so neither group can point a finger at the other. Scripture is clear that all have sinned and fall short of the glory of God (Romans 3:23). For Christians to imply that God has rejected Israel for her sins but will not reject them for theirs is self-righteous and judgmental.

In addition, covenant faithfulness is part of God's character. If He were to reject Israel and break His covenant with them because of their sin and disobedience, He would be morally obligated to break His covenant with the church for their sin and disobedience, and replace them with someone else as well, because He is a just God and cannot show favoritism. This would result in a never-ending cycle of God breaking His covenants and making new ones with different people groups.

But that is not the case. The God we serve is, by His very nature, faithful, even when we are unfaithful. He is a covenant-keeping God. To even imply that He breaks His covenants when we are unfaithful would be an attack on His character and the moral foundation of who He is.

Thankfully, God has not rejected Israel, as Paul the apostle so clearly and emphatically says: "Has God cast away His people? Certainly not! For I also am an Israelite, of the seed of Abraham, of the tribe of Benjamin. God has not cast away His people whom He foreknew" (Romans 11:1–2).

To further establish this point, Paul says in Romans 11:29, "The gifts and the calling of God are irrevocable." Although this Scripture is often quoted from the pulpit to demonstrate that once someone is called by God to be an evangelist or a pastor, that call is never revoked, this is not the application according to the context. Paul is saying here that the call of God on Israel as a people (the Jews) will never and can never be revoked. This is another key Scripture that destroys the Replacement Theology fallacy.

Because God has not broken His eternal covenant with the Jewish people, we can be assured as believers that He will never break His eternal covenant with us either. As Jeremiah goes on to say in describing the new covenant, "I will forgive their wicked-ness and will remember their sins no more" (31:34 NIV). I am eternally grateful that we serve a God who forgives our sins and keeps His covenants!

- It breeds spiritual elitism.

The unbiblical doctrine of Replacement Theology is a hindrance to fulfilling God's blueprint for the Great Commission because it breeds arrogance toward the Jewish people.

If Christians think that God has rejected Israel and that Jews no longer have a part in God's plan, the furthest thing from their minds will be trying to reach them with the gospel and the love of Jesus. They will be fine with letting the Jews perish while they—the "new Israel," God's current chosen people—go merrily on their way to heaven. This doctrine breeds a kind of spiritual elitism, with one group of people looking down on another based solely on them being born as Jews. One could go so far as to call this a form of "spiritual Nazism."

People who embrace this doctrine are unknowingly fulfilling Bible prophecy by ignoring the prophetic warning in Romans 11:17–21 (NIV).

> If some of the branches have been broken off, and you, though a wild olive shoot, have been grafted in among the others and now share in the nourishing sap from the olive root, do not consider yourself to be superior over those other branches. If you do, consider this: You do not support the root, but the root supports you. You will say then, "Branches were broken off so that I could be grafted in." Granted. But they were broken off because of unbelief, and you stand by faith. Do not be arrogant, but tremble. For if God did not spare the natural branches, he will not spare you either.

These passages warn Gentile believers not to become arrogant toward their Jewish brethren, who are not seeing the light of the gospel as a nation at this point. The wild branches (Gentiles) should not boast against the natural branches (the Jews).

God warns the Gentiles against feeling superior over the Jews, but he also says the Jews should not boast in their position as natural descendants of Abraham. Because God is fair, He judged the Jews for their unbelief. But He will judge the Gentiles for their arrogance if they boast against the Jews.

Paul brings his point to a conclusion with this admonition:

> Consider therefore the kindness and sternness of God: sternness to those who fell, but kindness to you, provided that you continue in his kindness. Otherwise, you also will be cut off. And if they do not persist in unbelief, they will be grafted in, for God is able to graft them in again. After all, if you were cut out of an olive tree that is wild by nature, and contrary to nature were grafted into a cultivated olive tree, how much more readily will these, the natural branches, be grafted into their own olive tree! (Romans 11:22–24 NIV)

Paul is admonishing all of us to maintain a humble attitude and a posture of gratitude for our salvation, which none of us has earned, worked for, or achieved by our own righteousness; it is the free gift of God. Romans 5:18 says, "As through one man's offense judgment came to all men, resulting in condemnation, even so through one Man's righteous act *the free gift* came to all men, resulting in justification of life" (emphasis added).

If Gentiles remain arrogant toward their Jewish brethren, they are in danger of being cut off too. Both Gentiles and Jews come into the kingdom by faith alone, and they stand by faith alone. All believers are admonished to maintain a humble attitude before God. First Peter 5:6 says, "Humble yourselves under the mighty hand of God, that He may exalt you in due time." We are all in the kingdom by faith through grace, and not by our own merits or righteousness.

Jews should not trust in their heritage to save them, even though we are ancestors of Abraham and the apple of God's eye (Zechariah 2:8). And Gentiles should not boast against the Jews and see them as rejected by God for all they have done wrong.

Ephesians 2:14 says that God has destroyed "the dividing wall of hostility" (NIV) between Jews and Gentiles, making "one new man from the two" (v. 15). Let us not rebuild that wall of hostility that Jesus died to take away. Instead, let us honor His sacrifice on the cross by showing the world that Jesus died to unite us into one new man. In the end this is what will save the world and bring people to God—if we have true love for one another and honor one another above ourselves.

HINDRANCE #5. DUAL-COVENANT THEOLOGY

This theology is the belief that Jews are saved through the Mosaic and Abrahamic covenants, while Christians are saved through the new covenant; therefore, Jews do not need to believe in Jesus to be saved.

This doctrine is as unbiblical as Replacement Theology. And it is yet another hindrance to fulfilling God's blueprint for the Great Commission.

The new covenant was made with Israel, and without it Jews cannot be saved, just as Gentiles cannot be saved apart from the sacrifice of Jesus on the cross. What an affront this belief is to the atoning work of Calvary, where Jesus laid down His life for the sins of Israel and the sins of the whole world.

Here are some of the reasons many Christians have embraced this ridiculous notion of Dual-Covenant Theology:

- They feel a general sense of guilt and shame over the Holocaust, and Christian anti-Semitism in general, and the silence of the church in the face of it. So they attempt to overcompensate for these abuses by saying Jews don't need Jesus to be saved. I have found this concept to be especially prevalent among German Christians.
- They have a sense of guilt and shame over centuries of Jewish persecution. So they adopt this extreme reaction in the opposite direction

to try to prove that Christians really do love the Jews and do not merely want to proselytize or convert them.

- It provides an easy way out of witnessing to Jews. Sharing the gospel with them can be challenging, and many don't want to put forth the effort required to reach out to Jews with the gospel, especially since it often comes with opposition and persecution, which is uncomfortable.

Here are the main reasons Dual-Covenant Theology produces bad fruit:

- If Christians think that Jews are already saved by their own separate covenant with God, they will never share the gospel with them. As a result, many Jewish people will perish without knowing their Messiah.
- It invalidates the need for all Jewish ministry in the church, as well as the thousands of people over the centuries who have dedicated their lives to reach the Jews with the gospel.
- It causes confusion among Christians, who are not presenting a united front to the Jewish community, and among the Jews, who are hearing some believers say they need Jesus to be saved while others say it is not necessary.

This doctrine might make some Christians feel better about themselves. But it is hurting the cause of Jewish evangelism and keeping Jews from their rightful spiritual inheritance in the kingdom.

HINDRANCE #6. WRONG INTERPRETATION OF ROMANS 11:26

Romans 11:26 says, "And so all Israel will be saved, as it is written: 'The Deliverer will come out of Zion, and He will turn away ungodliness from Jacob.'"

Many Christians who don't want to share the gospel with Jews for fear of offending them use this Scripture to justify their stance. Since all Jews are going to be saved anyway (according to their interpretation of this verse), there is no need to preach the gospel to them.

This verse could be interpreted that way if you didn't look at the context and what the rest of the Scriptures say about the issue of Jews needing Jesus to be saved.

For example, John 3:36 says, "He who believes in the Son has everlasting life; and he who does not believe the Son shall not see life, but the wrath of God abides on him." Jesus plainly told the Jewish leaders that if they died without believing in Him, they would "die in their sins" (John 8:24) and therefore perish—not because they were Jewish, but because they rejected the only one who could save them.

When Jesus said, "I am the way, the truth, and the life. No one comes to the Father except through Me" (John 14:6), He was speaking to His Jewish disciples, not to Gentiles. He was telling the Jews that without Him they could never have a relationship with the Father.

When Peter said, "Salvation is found in no one else, for there is no other name under heaven given to mankind by which we must be saved" (Acts 4:12 NIV), He was addressing the Jewish high priests and elders, the spiritual elite of the Jewish community, not Gentiles (even though this principle applies to them as well).

There are dozens more biblical examples that illustrate this point. Clearly, according to Jesus and Paul and all the other writers of the New Testament, Jews need to believe in Jesus to be saved.

HINDRANCE #7. WRONG ESCHATOLOGY

Because of a warped end-time eschatology, many Christians believe that God has placed a veil over the hearts and minds of the Jews so they can't be saved until after the rapture of the church, which will take place either at the beginning of the great seven-year tribulation or in the middle of the seven years. They say at the "rapture," the true church will be taken out of the world, and the Jews will be left to fend for themselves as the Antichrist tries to annihilate them in a manner similar to Hitler.

The prophet Jeremiah referred to this season as a time of great testing for Israel, when God will deal directly with the Jews to bring them back to himself. In this season God will release 144,000 Jewish evangelists, who will bring the gospel to Israel and the rest of the world in the midst of great distress, including beheadings and mass killings of those who refuse to worship the beast mentioned in Revelation.

I am not trying to invalidate any person's beliefs about how the end times will play out. Personally, I do believe in the rapture of the church, and Scripture is clear about a seven-year tribulation period. What I have a problem with is the view that while the Jews are being slaughtered and trying to singlehandedly take on the Antichrist (a man who will be even worse than Hitler), the Gentile church will be enjoying heaven, blissfully out of harm's way. According to this eschatology, only after the rapture of the church will the veil of blindness finally be removed, and then Jews will begin to get saved . . . even though the Antichrist would behead them for their faith if they were caught. What a convenient teaching— especially if you're not Jewish!

Not surprisingly, I have never heard a Jewish believer endorse this teaching. The fact that there are Jewish believers in the world today, myself included, shoots this doctrine in the head.

The fruit of the belief that Jews cannot be saved until after the rapture is that people don't share the gospel with Jews because they don't see the point in it. They base this stance on Scriptures like 2 Corinthians 3:14–15: "Their minds were blinded. For until this day the same veil remains unlifted in the reading of the Old Testament, because the veil is taken away in Christ. But even to this day, when Moses is read, a veil lies on their heart."

And yet, the very next verse says, "Nevertheless whenever one turns to the Lord, the veil is taken away" (v. 16). When a Jew is open to the truth of the gospel, the veil is removed and he will see Jesus as the Messiah revealed in the Old Testament Scriptures.

The idea that God has blinded the Jews so that they cannot be saved until after the rapture implies that God has predetermined some Jews to go to hell while others are predetermined to go to heaven, and they have absolutely no say in the matter. This makes God equivalent to Dr. Mengele, the infamous Nazi known as the "Angel of Death." He would send some Jews to the gas chambers on the left and others to work on the right, and they wouldn't know which line they were in until it was too late.

I feel sorry for Christians who have such a morbid view of God.

I feel even worse for all the people who have not received the gospel as a result of this kind of dogma, which for centuries has made the church largely irrelevant and ineffective in reaching the world for Jesus.

I do believe that Christians will be "caught up" as taught in 1 Thessalonians 4:16–17:

> The Lord Himself will descend from heaven with a shout, with the voice of an archangel, and with the trumpet of God. And the dead in Christ will rise first. Then we who are alive and remain shall be caught up together with them in the clouds to meet the Lord in the air. And thus we shall always be with the Lord.

I do not, however, believe that only Gentiles will be caught up, while all the Jews will be left behind to suffer the wrath of the Antichrist, because Scripture does not teach that. All people who have accepted Jesus as their Messiah, both Jews and Gentiles, will be caught up to be with the Lord and will be with Him forever.

So, what does Romans 11:26 mean when it says that "all Israel will be saved?" No other nation is guaranteed salvation, making this quite an amazing promise.

If we look at the big picture of eschatology and God's dealings with Israel, the Scriptures seem to point to a day of national repentance for Israel. Zechariah 12:10 says, "I will pour on the house of David and on the inhabitants of Jerusalem the Spirit of grace and supplication; then they will look on Me whom they pierced. Yes, they will mourn for Him as one mourns for his only son, and grieve for Him as one grieves for a firstborn." This verse is quoted in John 19:37, indicating that Jesus' death on the cross was a fulfillment of this prophecy.

Zechariah goes on to say, in verse 12, that "the land shall mourn," implying a national repentance over the rejection of the Messiah when they realize who Jesus is. Clearly this has not happened yet but is still to come.

This passage then names all the tribes of Israel that will mourn, including the house of David and the house of Levi. Verse 14 (NIV) adds, "and all the rest of the clans and their wives." The entire nation of Israel will one day repent over the one "whom they pierced."

Zechariah 13:1 says, "On that day a fountain will be opened to the house of David and the inhabitants of Jerusalem, to cleanse them from sin and impurity." The phrase "on that day" denotes an actual time when all Jews will be cleansed from sin and impurity.

This part of the prophecy will be fulfilled after a time of great tribulation, during which all the other nations will gather against Jerusalem to destroy her, and the Lord himself will come to destroy them. (See Zechariah 12:1–9.) As a result of this national repentance, the Lord will make even "the feeblest among them" (v. 8 NIV) like David in battle, until all the enemies of Israel are utterly destroyed.

Romans 11:26 does not say that every Jew who ever lived will automatically be saved, but that on the day when Jesus returns after the great tribulation, every Jew alive on the earth at that time will believe in Jesus and therefore be saved.

I would rather stand with Israel and have God on my side than stand with the masses who are incensed against Israel and be annihilated.

Zechariah 13:2 (NIV) says, "'On that day, I will banish the names of the idols from the land, and they will be remembered no more,' declares the Lord Almighty."

Sadly, there is currently a lot of idolatry in the land of Israel, as it is a largely secular nation. The New Age movement is very popular there, as are Eastern religions. But on this day of national repentance, all Israel will be cleansed from their sin, every idol will be removed from the land, and only the God of Israel will be worshipped. Yeshua the Messiah will rule and reign for a thousand years from Jerusalem, as prophesied in the Scriptures (Revelation 20:6). On that day there will be no more persecution of messianic Jews by their Jewish brethren, because every Jew alive on earth at that time will be a believer. How I long for that day!

Paul the apostle says in Romans 11:5, "So then, at this present time there is a remnant according to the election of grace." There has always been a remnant of Jewish believers throughout history. Even in the days of Elijah, when he thought he was the only Jewish believer in the world, God told him He had reserved seven thousand people who had not bowed the knee to Baal (1 Kings 19:18).

It has never been, nor will it ever be, a waste of time to bring the gospel to the Jewish people. Perhaps the Jewish person you have been witnessing to and praying for may be another Paul the apostle, who will change the world!

The time is coming when there will be a huge national revival among the Jews. In fact, we are seeing the firstfruits of it now. There are more than one hundred messianic congregations in Israel today and hundreds more around the world. There are more Jewish believers on earth today than ever before.

Thank God for the Gentile believers who love the Jews and are reaching out to them with the good news of their Messiah— those who refuse to believe the demonic doctrine that Jews can't be saved until after the rapture, or the false message that the Jews have been blinded by God and therefore cannot see or understand the gospel message. I thank God every day for Christians who believe that no one person is beyond the loving and graceful arms of God.

HINDRANCE #8. REVELATION VS. PROPAGATION

Another unbiblical teaching comes, surprisingly, from someone who is a major supporter of standing with Israel. (It is not necessary to mention this person by name, because my goal is not to expose any individual but rather to address false teachings that have had a damaging effect on Jewish evangelism.) This person claims that while Gentiles are saved by propagation (the preaching of the gospel), Jews are saved only by divine revelation (citing the example of Paul the apostle's vision of Jesus), and concludes that therefore it isn't necessary to preach the gospel to them.

This concept is contrary to Scripture. With the exception of Paul, almost all of the Jews who were saved in the first century came to know Jesus through the preaching of the gospel.

Yet many Gentiles of today cling to this approach because it allows them to abdicate the responsibility of sharing the gospel with their Jewish friends. It shifts the full responsibility of preaching the gospel to God, even though Jesus clearly put the Great Commission into our hands. I see this as a cop-out from what God has called us to do as Christians.

If it is God's responsibility to save the Jews through revelation in the form of dreams and visions, Peter must have been disobedient when he preached to thousands of Jews on the day of Pentecost, when more than three thousand souls were saved (Acts 2:41). This discounts all the times recorded in Scripture when multitudes of Jews were saved through the preaching of the gospel by Paul, Apollos, and many others.

HINDRANCE #9. FRIENDSHIP EVANGELISM

Sadly, many Christians feel that they must make a choice: either they can be friends with Jewish people or they can share the gospel with them, as if the two options are incompatible. In fact, the opposite is true.

Many Christians say they don't actively share their faith with their Jewish friends, they just love them. But is that love? If you see a friend headed toward a thousand-foot cliff, will you just "love" them until they fall off and die an untimely death?

In my experience, Jewish people greatly appreciate honesty right up front. Let your Jewish friends know that they need Jesus as their Messiah and you want them to accept him because you love them. But then let them know that your friendship with them is unconditional; it is not based on whether or not they accept Jesus.

If you befriend people solely with the hope of sharing Jesus with them after you have won their trust, they will feel used and betrayed when you do eventually share the gospel with them, because they will think you had a hidden agenda all along. You'll end up losing those friends because they'll feel you were being deceptive. You will also turn them off from the gospel because they'll see Christians as dishonest people.

I have a great relationship with my mother, who is not yet a believer. Of course she is Jewish, as is all my extended family. But she is one of my greatest supporters. One day, someone asked her what I do when I travel to various countries around the world, and she answered, "He evangelizes!" She knows that wherever I go I preach the gospel and win people to Jesus. That is all she has seen me do for over twenty-nine years, and she thinks that's normal behavior for any believer. And she's right—it should be normal.

Because I am honest and up front about what I believe, I have many Jewish friends who are not believers. In fact, I have more Jewish friends who are not believers than those who are. They find my approach refreshing.

I have what I call an "open agenda." Of course I want everyone I know to accept Jesus and be saved. But my relationships are not contingent on that. That is why I have so many Jewish friends. They know they can trust me.

We need to share our faith with our Jewish friends naturally, being sensitive to the Holy Spirit's prompting and letting him show us how and when to share with them. Romans 10:14–15 says, "How then shall they call on Him in whom they have not believed? And how shall they believe in Him of whom they have not heard? And how shall they hear without a preacher? And how shall they preach unless they are sent? As it is written: 'How beautiful are the feet of those who preach the gospel of peace!'"

Obviously, God is not saying that everyone who shares the gospel with a Jewish person has beautifully manicured feet and gorgeous toenails. He is referring to the fact that his blessing and favor are on those who bring the gospel to the Jewish people in a tangible way.

The most blessed people I know on the earth are those who either share the gospel directly with Jewish people or support Jewish ministries that reach Jews with the gospel. If you do that, you are guaranteed God's full support and blessing. I believe that reaching the lost sheep of the house of Israel is on the top of God's agenda. When you support his cause, he will support yours. I can attest to that through almost three decades of Jewish ministry.

I am not saying that God's love for you is based on how well you support Jewish ministries or preach the gospel to the Jews. But you will experience his blessing, protection, and nearness like never before if you support that which is dearest to his heart, which is reaching out to his beloved, the apple of his eye.

HINDRANCE #10. NO UNDERSTANDING OF TARGET EVANGELISM

The next major hindrance to fulfilling God's blueprint for the Great Commission is a subtle one, but perhaps even more of a hindrance to Jewish evangelism than the blatant ones. This is an apathetic, wishy-washy approach to reaching the Jews. Not having a clear strategy and plan to reach the Jews is really just another way of saying we have no real interest in reaching them.

The vast majority of saved Jews are not initially exposed to the gospel by fellow Jews or even through the messianic movement, but primarily through devoted, loving Christian neighbors or friends in the workplace. Most Jews will never go to a church or messianic synagogue to hear the gospel. Their Christian friends and coworkers are the only connections to Jesus and the gospel they have.

That is why I have spoken with hundreds of pastors over the years, asking them to allow me to help equip their body to reach

the Jewish community in their area. I've told them that even
if there were just five people in their churches who loved the
Jews and prayed for Israel, I would be happy to teach a Sunday
school class on how to effectively reach the Jews. For even greater
impact, I've offered to speak with the whole church about God's
passionate heart for the salvation of Israel.

In the early years when I was just getting established in my
ministry to the Jews, I had a full-time job to support my family
so I could do this free of charge. Whenever I met with a pastor
who didn't know me, I made it very clear that I did not require an
honorarium. My driving motive and my consuming passion was
for the salvation of my people, and I didn't want anything to get in
the way of reaching them.

Sadly, the most common response I got from pastors was
"We reach all people with the gospel. We don't focus on any one
particular group."

This "one size fits all" approach is often a death blow to
reaching any Jews with the gospel. It isn't even biblical. Paul the
apostle said, "I have become all things to all men, that I might by
all means save some" (1 Corinthians 9:22). In verse 20 of the same
chapter he said, "To the Jews I became as a Jew, that I might win
Jews."

Most pastors are unaware of how foreign the Christian church
culture is to the Jewish people. There are strong traditions and
practices in Christian churches that are the absolute antithesis of
Jewish culture and therefore a strong turnoff to Jews. If we truly
love the people we are trying to reach with the gospel, we will
remove every kind of offense or potential stumbling block that
might keep them from accepting Jesus.

The messianic services at Gateway Church in Southlake,
Texas (which I led for almost nine years), were held in a renovated
supermarket, so it doesn't look like either a church or a synagogue.
It was a nice building, and everything is done with excellence. But
it was a neutral location. We don't have any crosses on the inside
or outside. We do have messianic worship, and in every service
we sing the Shema, which is our common statement of faith as
Christians and Jews. Based on Deuteronomy 6:4, we declare,
"Hear, O Israel: The Lord our God, the Lord is one!" We call Jesus

by his Hebrew name, Yeshua, and always say Messiah instead of Christ. And the worship is powerful and full of life.

When Christians speak to Jews about receiving Jesus Christ as their Lord and Savior, I always cringe. Not because I object to people sharing their faith. But because Jews have been called "Christ killers" for centuries, so the term Christ is offensive to them. Most Jews have no idea that Christ is the Greek word for Messiah or "anointed one." If Christians stop talking Greek and start telling their Jewish friends that Jesus is the promised Messiah of Israel, whom they have been waiting for all these centuries, at least you'll both be talking the same language.

Christians often present the gospel in a churchy, preachy kind of way that Jewish people find irrelevant. This usually happens because Christians have little interaction with Jewish people and culture, so they don't tailor their messages in a way that is relevant to Jews.

Paul, the master evangelist of his time, said we should become all things to all men in order to win as many people as possible. In 1 Corinthians 9:20, he said, "I became as a Jew that I might win Jews." In verse 22 he adds, "To the weak I became as weak, that I might win the weak. I have become all things to all men, that I might by all means save some."

Sadly, this is largely a lost art. Many preachers don't have a clue how to reach someone outside of their cultural context. I shudder to think how many souls have been lost for heaven because of this strategic mistake. Whether it is deliberate or not, the results are tragic. Our approach to an ever-evolving and always-changing society has to become more relevant.

Politicians use this strategy to win elections. Why are we not using it to win souls for eternity? As Proverbs 11:30 says, "He that wins souls is wise."

PRACTICAL APPLICATION

I was born in Kwazulu, Natal, near Durban in South Africa. I was raised in the Orthodox Jewish traditions and educated at private Jewish schools, where we said prayers in Hebrew for one hour every morning and I lay tefillin (what Jesus called phylacteries in the New Testament). I was raised almost exclusively in Jewish neighborhoods and had very little exposure to Gentiles until my later teen years. Even then I knew only a few South African Gentiles, none from any other cultures or nations. Yet now I have preached the gospel in twenty-three countries, including Indonesia, which is over 90 percent Muslim and a hotbed for radical Islam. I ministered in Argentina for more than twelve years. I've ministered in Italy, Odessa, the Ukraine, South Korea, and many more countries. Each of these cultures is foreign to me, yet in every one of these nations I have connected with the people and they treat me like one of their own.

In many of these places, I have won many souls to the Lord in just a single visit. Yet in the natural, I have nothing in common with them. How can this be accomplished? I follow the principle Paul lived by: to become all things to all men.

In Indonesia, I preached wearing one of their hand-woven shirts, and I opened with a greeting in their language. In Argentina, I told my hosts how much I enjoyed their delicious steaks and *dulce de leche*, and the audience appreciated the effort I made to engage them and their customs. The smallest attempts to show people you love their culture and are willing to engage with them will go a long way. It can be the difference between souls going to heaven or to hell. If you really love people, you will do whatever it takes to reach them with the gospel in a way that is relevant to them.

The retail and marketing world embraces the term *target market*. A company that wants to sell a product or service needs to know their target audience and have a strategy to penetrate it. For example, if you wanted to promote a new brand of women's perfumes, you wouldn't advertise in the rifle section of a hunting store. You'd be more likely to advertise at Victoria's Secret. Yet the world is much wiser at marketing their products than Christians are at promoting the gospel.

I realize that Jesus is not a product. He is the priceless, matchless Son of God, who offers us forgiveness, eternal life, peace, righteousness, and "joy inexpressible and full of glory" (1 Peter 1:8). But since we have the only message that offers lasting and eternal solutions to all of life's problems and needs, we should be able to do a far better job at promoting it. The message is sacred and unchanging: the eternal gospel of our salvation. But we can change the packaging to make it more appealing to a wider range of people. I am not talking about watering down the gospel message, God forbid! But I am talking about speaking to people in a way that they understand that they are so valuable to God that if they were the only person on the planet Jesus would have died for them.

If we don't have a strategy to reach our "target audience," we won't be successful. Any person who's been in marketing for any length of time could tell us that. So why don't we get this in the church?

We must have a specific, God-given strategy or we'll be setting ourselves up for failure, whether it is for Jewish ministry or any other kind of ministry. If we want to reach Jews with the gospel, we need to present Jesus to them in a Jewish way, as the promised Messiah. We have to tailor our approach to make the gospel relevant and attractive to them. And as I have mentioned this can be done successfully without in any way compromising the integrity of the gospel message.

Let us remove every obstacle to fulfilling God's blueprint for the Great Commission. Let's put aside every excuse for not bringing the gospel to the Jews and work together to reach God's chosen people.

Part Three

How to Pray for Israel

Prayer is the catalyst for any major move of God. Without it, we can accomplish little, if anything, for the kingdom. Prayer is a major key for any successful ministry, and I cannot emphasize enough how crucial it is for Jewish ministry.

WHAT TO PRAY FOR

In Romans 10:1, Paul the apostle said, "My heart's desire and prayer to God for Israel is that they may be saved." At that time, Israel was not an independent nation; rather, it was under Roman occupation and domination. When Paul spoke about Israel, he was referring not only to Jews living in Israel but also to those who were living in the Gentile nations outside of their homeland (in what is now referred to as the Diaspora). In this prayer, Paul is clearly reflecting God's heart, which is that all Jews everywhere would be saved.

Many people today are praying for the country of Israel, which is very important, but they forget to pray for the salvation of Jews worldwide. About half of the Jewish people in the world today live outside the land of Israel, and God is just as concerned about reaching them with the gospel. He wants us to have the same passion when we pray for the Jews in North America, South America, South Africa, and all over Eastern and Western Europe as we do for those living in Israel.

Paul's admonition in Romans 10:1 gives us a solid foundation on which to bring the gospel to Jewish people today. Jews need Jesus, their Messiah, in order to be saved. The same is true for Gentiles as well.

Whenever prayer for Israel is mentioned, many Christians think of Psalm 122:6, which says, "Pray for the peace of Jerusalem: 'May they prosper who love you.'" Verse 9 goes on to say, "For the sake of the house of the LORD our God, I will seek your prosperity" (NIV). There is an undeniable link in Scripture between the health and prosperity of the local church, which is "the house of the LORD our God," and their stand for the well-being of Jerusalem and the Jewish people. No wonder there are so many spiritually unhealthy churches around the world, when so many Christians believe they have replaced Israel and that God's plans for Israel are now only for the church. They don't realize that God promises to bless those churches and individuals who love and pray for His chosen people.

When Christians follow this Scripture's encouragement, their prayers tend to focus on the city of Jerusalem. They pray for its peace, which, in the minds of most, means the absence of war. There is nothing wrong with this thinking, especially since Jerusalem has seen more war than any other city on earth. (It has been conquered and occupied about forty times over the centuries.) But Jerusalem will not see true peace until the Prince of Peace, Jesus, rules and reigns in her midst. So when we pray for the peace of Jerusalem, we should be praying for the rule and reign of the Messiah to be established.

While that will only come to pass fully at the second coming, the Jewish people can find peace in their hearts today if they embrace their Messiah Yeshua. This is where true peace begins. In John 14:27, Jesus told the first Jewish disciples in Jerusalem, "Peace I leave with you, My peace I give to you; not as the world gives do I give to you. Let not your heart be troubled, neither let it be afraid."

When we pray for the peace of Jerusalem, we are praying ultimately for the gospel of peace to come to the city and to the land, to the hearts of Jews and Arabs alike. The only hope for long-term peace in Israel is for both Jews and Arabs to worship the one true God through Jesus the Messiah.

There are congregations in Israel that meet weekly, where Jews and Arabs worship God side by side without conflict or strife. But the secular media doesn't talk about that. They prefer to focus on the division there, because that makes for more sensational headlines.

While it is certainly important to pray for physical peace in Israel—for the absence of war and for safety and protection of all those who live in the land—the most important thing to pray for is the salvation of the Jewish people. Ultimately, the flourishing and full restoration of the land of Israel is intrinsically intertwined with her spiritual condition. Throughout the Bible, we see that when Israel was walking close to God as a nation, her physical boundaries expanded. Toward the end of King David's reign and through much of King Solomon's reign, the borders of Israel were huge. Militarily, no one could even come close to defeating her. But when she was far from God, her physical borders shrank and she regularly came under attack.

The same truth stands today, though the Bible is clear that the Jews will never again be removed from their land. Amos 9:15 (NIV) says, "'I will plant Israel in their own land, never again to be uprooted from the land I have given them,' says the LORD your God."

I believe that a national revival in Israel will ultimately result in more secure borders and a much larger territory than they enjoy today. When the Jews turn back to God through their Messiah

Yeshua, God will defend, protect, and expand her borders. The Scriptures are clear that "He who watches over Israel will neither slumber nor sleep"(Psalm 121:4 NIV).

The church today needs to invest in concentrated prayer for the spiritual renewal of Israel. They also need to support the body of Messiah in the land of Israel, as Jewish believers in local congregations will be the main agents for revival in their nation. I believe with all my heart that as the worldwide body of Messiah prays diligently and earnestly for Israel's spiritual restoration, God will correspondingly restore her physical borders. Fighting for the physical land while ignoring the spiritual root of the problem is like putting a Band- Aid over a wound without first applying a healing balm.

HOW TO PRAY

The Bible says that it is not God's will for anyone to perish; rather, His desire is that all would come to repentance (2 Peter 3:9). That includes both Jews and Gentiles. Scripture also says, "The god of this world has blinded the minds of the unbelieving, so they might not see the light of the Good News of the glory of Messiah, who is the image of God" (2 Corinthians 4:4 TLV).

The Devil blinds the minds of unbelievers. So part of our prayers for the lost, both Jews and Gentiles, should include spiritual warfare. Through prayer we can bind the demonic strongholds that are blinding people from seeing the truth of the gospel.

In Matthew 12:29, Jesus said, "How can one enter a strong man's house and plunder his goods, unless he first binds the strong man? And then he will plunder his house." The first step in praying for the unsaved is to bind the Devil from blinding their minds. Jesus has given us the authority to do that in his name; in fact, He has commanded us to (Luke 10:19).

I hear many Christians today asking God to bind the Devil. But He has already given us the power to do that. Of course, we do it not in our authority or name, but in the authority and name of Jesus. Asking Him to do it for us is a cop-out from our God-given mandate to take authority over the evil one.

PRAYING SPECIFICALLY FOR THE JEWISH PEOPLE

Are we to pray any differently for Jewish people than for Gentiles? The surprising answer is yes.

In 2 Corinthians 3:14–16, Paul says, in regard to the children of Israel, that a "veil remains unlifted in the reading of the Old Testament, because the veil is taken away in Christ. Even to this day, when Moses is read, a veil lies on their heart. Nevertheless when one turns to the Lord, the veil is taken away."

I can personally testify to this. I was blind to the truth of the gospel as a Jew. But the first time I read Psalm 22, God lifted the "veil" for me and I saw Jesus almost immediately.

And yet, when I share Psalm 22 with other Jewish people, and ask them who they think it is talking about, I often get a blank stare. Some say maybe King David or some other Jewish person was describing his own suffering. Only a few get the connection between the words of Psalm 22 and the details of Jesus' crucifixion.

I believe the difference between those whose eyes are opened and those who remain blind is prayer. Of course free will is also involved. But faith-filled prayers can result in the removal of the veil so the Jewish people can see their Messiah in the Scriptures and also though dreams, visions, and supernatural revelation.

After the resurrection, when Jesus appeared to the disciples, Luke 24:45 (NIV) says, "Then he opened their minds so they could understand the Scriptures." Jesus was right in front of them, in the flesh, yet He still had to open their minds in order for them to understand the Scriptures and see Him in the Word. If that was the case for Jewish believers who were seeing Him in person, how much more should we be praying that God will open the eyes of unbelieving Jews who cannot see Him in their own Scriptures?

So when we pray for our Jewish friends and neighbors, we need to bind the Devil. But we also need to petition the God of Israel to remove the veil that lies over their hearts and minds.

COMBINE PRAYER WITH ACTION

For those Jews we come into contact with, whom God has placed along our paths, we should combine our prayers with action.

We can start by pointing them to the prophecies in the Old Testament, encouraging them to read the Scriptures for themselves. Then trust that as God removes the veil they will see the Messiah.

I cannot describe the joy that fills my heart whenever I watch a Jewish person read Psalm 22 for the first time and they realize they are reading a description of Jesus' crucifixion. As if scales are falling from their eyes, they can suddenly see clearly, much like Paul the apostle experienced in the physical realm (see Acts 9:18).

When I got saved, God gave me a special gift of faith to know that all of my immediate family would eventually be saved. Since none of them believed in Jesus, and all came from a traditional Jewish Orthodox background, that was a big deal! But nothing is too big for God (Luke 1:37).

And God has been true to His word. Over the last thirty years or so that I have been a believer, not one of my close family members has died without receiving Jesus as their Messiah (even though it has been a battle at times, to put it mildly).

My grandmother on my mother's side, whose name is Fruma, was raised in a very traditional Orthodox Jewish home in a small Jewish village in Lithuania called Kipuskis. She moved to South Africa at the age of twenty-six. There she met my grandfather Leslie, who was also from an Orthodox Jewish background.

My parents, my two sisters, and I enjoyed Shabbat dinner with my grandmother Fruma and grandfather Leslie every Friday night. When he found out that I had accepted Jesus as the Messiah, he instantly assumed that I had become part of the group of people who had persecuted and killed Jews over the centuries. In his opinion, the world was divided into two groups: "us" (the Jews) and "them" (the Christians). People were either one or the other; no one could be both. Even though I loved my people and Israel more than ever, in his eyes I had morphed overnight from one of "us" into one of "them."

His perspective was understandable. After all, he'd experienced pogroms in Lithuania firsthand. He'd seen women beaten and raped, and rabbis and other Jewish leaders maimed and killed, as part of a crusade to avenge the Jews for supposedly killing their Savior. Jesus told the Jews of his day, "The time will come when those who kill you will think that by doing this they are serving God" (John 16:2 GNT). That was certainly true of many of the professing Christians in my grandfather's time.

For the first few years after I became a believer, the tension between my grandparents and me was palpable. But over time, they saw that faith in Yeshua made me a better and more loving person, and the consistency of my life began to win over their hearts and minds.

What surprised them even more than my changed life was my increased love for and support of Israel and my Jewish brethren. I did not deny my Jewish roots, but rather embraced them even more. They saw that being a Jew and believing in the Jewish Messiah was not a contradiction but in fact a perfectly natural fit.

My grandfather gradually softened to the gospel. He even read books I gave him with testimonies of famous messianic Jews and the price they paid to bring the Messiah to their people. Though he maintained a tough exterior, he started warming up to me (and, more importantly, to the gospel).

One day, my grandmother Fruma came into the study, where I was reading, and I pointed her to Psalm 22 in her Tanach (the Hebrew Bible). After she read it, I asked her who she thought it was talking about. To my utter astonishment she immediately said, in her strong Yiddish accent, "Well, it is obviously talking about Jesus on the cross."

This was the first time my grandmother had ever read this Psalm, and she was not a believer in Jesus. But I had been praying for her salvation for about ten years, asking God to remove the veil and show her the Messiah.

Trying not to show my shock and excitement, I asked, "So you believe this passage is talking about Yeshua, the Messiah?"

"Well, yes," she answered matter-of-factly.

"Then what is stopping you from praying to receive Jesus as your Messiah?"

Her eyes widened and her back straightened. "Oh, I could never do that!"

"Why not?"

"What would my mother and my father think?"

My grandmother's parents had died in Lithuania about fifty years earlier. Yet she was concerned about their opinion of her—especially her mother, which just shows how strong the influence of a Jewish mama is. They can even dictate to you from the grave!

"It would be like betraying my family," she added.

"But Gran," I said, "Jesus is the Messiah of our people. This Psalm proves it."

Her shoulders slumped. "I know. But I just can't do what you're asking. It goes against everything I was brought up to believe."

Unable to fight Jewish family tradition, I left the room disappointed . . . yet more encouraged than ever to keep praying for my grandmother's salvation until I saw it with my own eyes.

Shortly after that, I emigrated to the US. While I was gone, my grandfather Leslie received Yeshua and later passed away. When I returned to South Africa, I visited my grandmother in a Jewish retirement home in Johannesburg. She was degenerating quickly and often did not recognize even close family members. But she recognized me immediately and was delighted to see me. Since I had been praying for her salvation, this miracle did not surprise me.

After embracing, chatting, and catching up with her, I ventured into more serious territory. "Gran, you know Papa is with the Lord in heaven because he was a believer in Jesus, don't you?"

"Ja," she said (Ja meaning "yes").

"Do you remember Psalm 22, which I shared with you years ago?"

"*Ja.*"

"Do you still believe that passage refers to Jesus on the cross?"

"*Ja.*"

"You want to be with Papa forever, don't you?"

"*Ja.*"

"So what is stopping you from praying to receive Yeshua into your heart?"

She shrugged. "Nothing is stopping me."

My heart leapt. "Gran, are you okay with me leading you in that prayer right now?"

"*Ja.*"

I took her hands and squeezed them gently. "Yeshua, I thank you that you are the promised Messiah of Israel and my Messiah. I thank you that you died for my sins and the sins of my people. I believe that you died and rose from the dead for me. I receive you into my heart in Yeshua's name. Amen." I recited that prayer one short phrase at a time, and my beloved gran repeated the words after me.

There is no way to describe how precious that moment was, when after nearly twenty years of sowing in prayer, I was able to lead my own flesh and blood to the Lord.

As I rejoiced with her, I told her that Yeshua would one day return to Israel to deliver the Jewish people as a nation and how they would all finally embrace their Messiah.

Her eyes filled with tears. "Geoffrey, you give me hope!"

My heart broke to think that my beloved grandmother had lived more than ninety years with no real hope in her life, just going through the motions. But in that moment, I felt as if God was speaking to me through her. Those five words changed my entire approach to ministering to my people. I realized that we need to offer them the only true, lasting, and eternal hope that is available to them: the hope of the gospel. This is not only a hope for deliverance from Israel's enemies, which will eventually come, but hope for redemption and a more abundant life in the here and now.

From that moment on, I no longer saw Jewish ministry as a difficult effort of arguing, debating, and trying to persuade them, but rather as an offering of hope to a people who have lived so long without one. Yeshua is the only solution to all their needs, as a nation and as individuals.

Knowing that I will someday be reunited with my grandparents in heaven, along with the other precious Jewish and Gentile souls I have led to the Lord, either directly or indirectly, makes all the struggle worthwhile!

THE NEXT GREAT MOVE OF GOD

Some people think that Jewish ministry is tough because Jews have so many obstacles and objections to the gospel. But when you are guided by the love of God, nothing is too difficult, because love brings down the thickest of walls and melts the hardest of hearts.

In my travels around the world over the past decade, I have seen a new openness to the gospel among the Jewish people. The spiritual restoration of Israel will ultimately usher in the second coming and the advent of the millennial reign of the Messiah. Zechariah 12:10–14 says:

> I will pour on the house of David and on the inhabitants of Jerusalem the Spirit of grace and supplication; then they will look on Me whom they pierced. Yes, they will mourn for Him as one mourns for his only son, and grieve for Him as one grieves for a firstborn. In that day there shall be a great mourning in Jerusalem, like the mourning at Hadad Rimmon in the plain of Megiddo. And the land shall mourn, every family by itself: the family of the house of David by itself, and their wives by themselves; the family of the house of Nathan by itself, and their wives by themselves; the family of the house of Levi by itself, and their wives by themselves; the family of

Shimei by itself, and their wives by themselves; all the families that
remain, every family by itself, and their wives by themselves.

This passage describes a season of national repentance in
Israel, where the Jewish people will finally realize that the one
who died on the cross and was pierced, the one they rejected,
came to save them and bring them hope. I believe this refers to
the second coming, when all of Israel will see Jesus' feet touch
down on the Mount of Olives, and the mountain will split in
two, dividing into east and west (Zechariah 12:14).

But I also believe this passage refers to a season we are enter-
ing into now. The above Scripture says that after God "pours on
the house of David and on the inhabitants of Jerusalem the Spirit
of grace and supplication," they will "look on [Him] whom they
pierced." This suggests the beginning of a national revival before
the second coming of Jesus.

This revival is a direct response to the prayers of thousands
of Christians around the world who are praying faithfully for
Israel's salvation. In every nation, pockets of Jews are considering the claims of Jesus and coming to believe in Him. More Jews
are becoming followers of Jesus now than we have seen since the
first century, when the church was founded by a group of Jewish
believers in Jerusalem.

Jeremiah Predicted This Revival

This worldwide spiritual awakening among the Jewish people
is evidence of the prophetic era in which we are living. In many
Scripture passages, God promised an end-times revival to the
Jewish people.

For example, Jeremiah 31:31 describes the covenant that God
will make with Israel:

The days are coming, says the Lord, when I will make a new covenant
with the house of Israel and with the house of Judah.

When we hear the words *new covenant* today, we don't usually think of Israel or the Jewish people. But they are the ones God originally made it with. This was so clear to the Jewish believers in the first century that the gospel was initially preached only to Jews. "Those who were scattered after the persecution that arose over Stephen traveled as far as Phoenicia, Cyprus, and Antioch, preaching the word to no one but the Jews only" (Acts 11:19). The early believers preached only to Jews because they understood the new covenant was made with Israel. They did not yet understand that it was for the Gentiles as well.

God elaborates on this new covenant with Israel in Jeremiah 31:33:

> This is the covenant that I will make with the house of Israel after those days, says the Lord: I will put My law in their minds, and write it on their hearts; and I will be their God, and they shall be My people.

Here God is saying that the law will be internalized on their hearts (when the Holy Spirit comes to live in them). No longer will they need to try to follow all the external requirements of the law as best they could. All believers experience this incredible gift now.

> No more shall every man teach his neighbor, and every man his brother, saying, "Know the Lord," for *they all shall know Me*, from the least of them to the greatest of them, says the Lord. For I will forgive their iniquity, and their sin I will remember no more (v. 34, emphasis added).

This Scripture is not only a description of the new covenant but also a prophecy that the day will come when all Israel shall be saved, from the greatest to the least, regardless of social stature, fame, or success in life. Not just the Levites or the prophets or the kings, but every Jewish person will have a personal relationship with God.

I am not saying that every Jew who has ever lived will automatically be saved. That would invalidate the need to preach the gospel to them, and it would nullify the Great Commission. But at Jesus' second coming, all Jews who are alive on the earth will see Him and believe in Him. As a precursor to that great event, it is prophesied there will be a mighty outpouring of the Holy Spirit on the people and the land. This is why we need to continue to pray for Israel's salvation.

Ezekiel Predicted This Revival

Ezekiel 37 also talks about this future spiritual awakening among the Jews. When the prophet was in a valley filled with dry bones, God asked him, "Son of man, can these bones live?" (v. 3). Ezekiel wisely answered, "O Lord God, You know," perhaps as a way to avoid giving the wrong answer.

God commanded Ezekiel to prophesy to the dry bones, which he did.

> And as I prophesied, there was a noise, and suddenly a rattling; and the bones came together, bone to bone. Indeed, as I looked, the sinews and the flesh came upon them, and the skin covered them over; but there was no breath in them (vv. 7–8).

In Scripture, breath (*ruach* in Hebrew) refers to the Spirit of God. Though the dry bones had been physically restored with healthy sinews, flesh, and skin, they were still spiritually dead.

So God told Ezekiel:

> Prophesy to the breath, prophesy, son of man, and say to the breath, "Thus says the Lord God: 'Come from the four winds, O breath, and breathe on these slain, that they may live'" (v. 9).

I believe the breath that comes "from the four winds" refers to a revival of prayer for the spiritual restoration of Israel among churches worldwide. Those prayers will ultimately usher in the

greatest move of God the world has ever seen. The Holy Spirit
will come into the hearts of Jewish people when they receive
Yeshua as their Messiah. There is no other way to receive the
Holy Spirit.

Ezekiel prophesied to the breath, in obedience to God's
command.

> And breath came into them, and they lived, and stood upon their feet,
> an exceedingly great army (v. 10).

Israel has long been known for the might of their military
forces. But in the future, they will be known for being "an exceed-
ingly great army" for the Lord and His kingdom.

Then God said to Ezekiel:

> Son of man, these bones are the *whole house of Israel*. They indeed say,
> "Our bones are dry, our hope is lost, and we ourselves are cut off!" (v. 11,
> emphasis added)

This graphic imagery fits the emaciated Jews during the
Holocaust, who were starved to the point where they looked
like skeletons. The Jewish families who lost close relatives and
extended family members in the concentration camps certainly
felt that their hope of a future was lost and that they had been
cut off.

God then told Ezekiel:

> Therefore prophesy and say to them, "Thus says the Lord God:
> 'Behold, O My people, I will open your graves and cause you to come
> up from your graves, and bring you into the land of Israel. Then you
> shall know that I am the Lord, when I have opened your graves,
> O My people, and brought you up from your graves'" (vv. 12–13).

In 1945, when soldiers liberated the concentration camps,
they noticed that some of the "corpses" showed signs of life. These

Jews literally came out of their graves. As their protruding bones were gradually restored, and ravaged flesh was revitalized, they began to look like humans again instead of corpses. God then brought them to the land of Israel to start new lives, thus specifically fulfilling this incredible prophecy.

I realize this passage of Scripture is mainly depicting Israel's barren spiritual condition and not alluding purely to physical starvation and bodies being left for dead in concentration camps. However, I believe the physical parallels are obvious.

God went on to promise:

> "I will put My Spirit in you, and you shall live, and I will place you in your own land. Then you shall know that I, the Lord, have spoken it and performed it," says the Lord (v. 14).

This clearly refers to the rebirth of the nation of Israel, which happened in May of 1948, at a time when it looked like all hope was lost.

As wonderful and miraculous as the physical restoration of the Jews and the rebirth of the nation of Israel are, the best is yet to come.

Israel today is a mostly secular society, with no "breath" in them. The next great miracle for the Jewish people will be when the breath of God, the Ruach Hakodesh (the Holy Spirit) enters into them.

The prophetic promises for Israel's spiritual restoration will come to pass just as surely as the promises for their physical restoration did, even though it seems impossible in the natural.

Jesus shared this truth with one of the leaders of Israel in His day. Nicodemus came to Him by night and said, "Rabbi, we know that You are a teacher come from God; for no one can do these signs that You do unless God is with him." (John 3:2).

Jesus answered, "Most assuredly, I say to you, unless one is born again, he cannot see the kingdom of God" (v. 3). At first, this statement seems disconnected from Nicodemus's comment.

But Nicodemus replied, "How can a man be born when he is old? Can he enter a second time into his mother's womb and be born?" (v. 4).

Jesus replied, "That which is born of the flesh is flesh, and that which is born of the Spirit is spirit" (v. 6).

Of course, as believers today, we know that Jesus was referring to the new birth, or what we call being born again. But there is another implication that is less obvious at first glance.

Jesus was addressing one of the leaders of the Jewish people in Israel. When He said, "That which is born of the flesh is flesh," He was referring to the Jews being the natural descendants of Abraham. So in addition to telling Nicodemus how he could be saved personally, He was also talking about the survival of His people. He was saying that it's not enough for the Jews to be natural descendants of Abraham and to trust in that alone. They also need to become spiritual descendants of Abraham by becoming born again by the Holy Spirit and coming alive spiritually. Jesus was prophesying the ultimate solution for Israel: their spiritual rebirth.

If Nicodemus had taken those words to heart, who knows how things might have worked out differently!

But the only way this can happen is for the Jews to embrace Yeshua as their Messiah.

This is where you and I come into the picture. By praying for the salvation of Israel, we can be directly involved in this great end-times move of God. We "prophesy to the breath" when we pray prophetically, according to God's Word, for the Holy Spirit to bring revival to the land and for the Jewish people around the world to turn back to the God of Israel through their Messiah.

KEEP UP THE GOOD WORK

More than any other event, the spiritual restoration of Israel will usher in the return of the Lord. We look forward to that day, promised in Romans 11:26–27, when all Israel will be saved, as it is written: "The Deliverer will come out of Zion, and He will turn away ungodliness from Jacob; for this is My covenant with them, when I take away their sins."

Through the salvation of the Jews, the greatest revival mankind has ever seen is about to be ushered in. But this will not happen by default as we idly stand by. It will happen in response to generations of prayers for the salvation of the lost sheep of the house of Israel, prayed by faithful believers who love the Jewish people.

Your prayers of faith for the peace of Jerusalem and the salvation of Israel are an essential part of this revival. They are the key to bringing these prophecies to pass. So don't ever give up.

Your prayers are not being ignored, nor are they in vain. They are going straight up to the throne room in heaven as sweet incense before God's throne. He hears your prayers, and He is answering them.

In my early years as a Jewish believer I would often hear a Gentile Christian share his or her testimony in this way. "My believing mother or grandmother, or aunt or uncle had been praying for me for many years and now I am saved in answer to their prayers." Remember that very few Jewish people have the luxury of believing relatives praying for them because for almost two thousand years we have been cut off from the gospel with the exception of a very small believing remnant. So God is calling you to be that believing aunt, uncle, grandmother or mother. Take it upon yourself to adopt at least one Jew as if they were your own family. Then pray for their salvation until you see them in the kingdom and serving the Lord. Thank you for praying and never giving up!

PART FOUR

HOW TO SHARE THE GOSPEL
WITH THE JEWISH PEOPLE

Christians often feel intimidated at the thought of bringing the gospel to the Jewish people. As a result, few end up sharing their faith with them.

As it is human nature to not leave our comfort zones, sadly, Christians often overlook the Jewish people when it comes to the gospel. Though the oversight is mostly unintentional, churches tend to ignore the Jews as a people group when planning their outreach strategies. A friend of mine jokingly refers to this as "The Great Omission." Though he says it tongue-in-cheek, it has a sad ring of truth to it.

During the Holocaust, German citizens watched trains with thousands of Jews being shipped to death camps in cattle cars. They ate their meals in peace as they watched smoke pour out of the chimneys, not daring to contemplate where that smoke was coming from.

Eliezer Berkovits, a respected Jewish author, said this of the silence and passive stance of most of European Christendom during the Holocaust:

> After nineteen centuries of Christianity, the extermination of six
> million Jews, among them one and a half million children, carried
> out in cold blood in the very heart of Christian Europe, encouraged
> by the criminal silence of virtually all Christendom, including that
> of an infallible Holy Father in Rome, was the natural culmination of
> this bankruptcy. A straight line leads from the first act of oppression
> against the Jews and Judaism in the fourth century to the holocaust in
> the twentieth.[10]

The German Christians in Nazi-occupied countries could have saved at least some of the Jews . . . if they truly wanted to. After all, Oscar Schindler, a full-fledged Nazi, saved hundreds of Jewish lives. But because it would have been inconvenient, even dangerous, for them to acknowledge there was a Holocaust taking place on their doorstep, most Germans—even the Christian ones—let the Jews die.

Of course, there were some faithful Christians, like Corrie ten Boom, who saved Jewish lives at the risk of their own, sometimes paying the ultimate price. But these were the exception to the rule.

Today, many Christians know Jewish people, and some have close Jewish friends. They realize they need to share the gospel with them. But that would take them outside of their comfort zone. And they're afraid of offending them. So they avoid witnessing altogether. Instead, they maintain superficial friendships, hoping to quietly "love them to the Lord." As a result, many Jews are perishing without ever hearing that their beloved Messiah has come.

---

[10]Frank Talmage, *Disputation and Dialogue: Readings in the Jewish-Christian Encounter* (NJ: KTAV Publishing House, Inc., 1975), 287.

It's very disturbing to me that Christians would let their Jewish friends go to hell without hearing the gospel, merely to avoid a few moments of personal discomfort.

When I became a believer in Jesus, my immediate response was one of incredible joy at this indescribable gift. But my second reaction was anger toward Christians when I realized they had kept the Messiah of the Jewish people to themselves for centuries. I'd known thousands of professing Christians, but none of them had told me or my fellow Jews that our Messiah had come. Thus I remained ignorant of the gospel until a born-again Christian from Washington, DC, came all the way to Israel and shared the gospel with me.

I couldn't understand why no one had even told me before that Jesus, Yeshua, was a Jew. Did they not know? Did they not care? Had they not read Jesus' words in John 4:22, where He said that "salvation is of the Jews"?

Many Gentile Christians today choose to ignore the prophetic warning in Romans 11:18, which says, "Do not boast against the branches. But if you do boast, remember that you do not support the root, but the root supports you." If they really believed that the glorious salvation they enjoy came through the Jewish nation, they would be more actively engaged in bringing the gospel to their Jewish friends, neighbors, and coworkers.

A few months ago, I was ministering in South Africa, and a Zulu pastor who didn't even know me said to the congregation, "Don't you realize that if not for the Jewish people, you would not have the gospel? We owe them a debt of gratitude. I realize that the gospel is from God alone, but He chose to bring it to the world through the Jewish nation. He brought His Son into the world as a Jew, from the tribe of Judah, and He will return to rule and reign as the 'lion of the tribe of Judah' (Revelation 5:5). Jesus did not stop being a Jew just because He went to heaven."

I am no longer angry at Christians. I love them dearly. They are my brothers and sisters in the faith. But I hope that they will

develop a sense of accountability and love for their Jewish brethren that will lead to action steps to bring the gospel to them.

On a regular basis, I sit down with unsaved Jewish people
over a meal in a restaurant, or over a cup of coffee, or in my
office. I have met with Holocaust survivors who are wondering
if God really cares, Orthodox Jews who have questions about the
Messiah, secular Jews, and even some well-known rabbis who
have contacted me secretly. They all have one thing in common:
they are looking for spiritual answers.

In the following section, I will demystify some of the misconceptions many Christians have about the Jewish people and
the gospel. I will also share some practical tips that will make it
easy for believers to share their faith with their Jewish friends and
neighbors.

I will then discuss three simple principles that I have found
to be biblical cornerstones in bringing the gospel to the Jewish
people. By using these three principles over the last few decades,
I have led many Jewish people to the Lord. Of course, there is no
guaranteed formula to bring Jews to salvation, because we all have
freedom of choice. But these principles are extremely effective
with those who have an open heart to the truth.

MISCONCEPTIONS

Following are some misconceptions Christians tend to have about
Jewish people and what they believe . . . and what our response to
these misconceptions should be.

Misconception #1. Jewish People Are Biblically Literate

Christians are often shocked when they discover that many Jewish
people do not have much knowledge of the Scriptures. Many
assume that because the Bible was written by Jews, the Jewish
people of today must believe in it and accept it as the inspired
Word of God. The truth is, in many countries, the vast majority of Jews are culturally Jewish but not strongly religious. Unless
they were raised orthodox or attended Jewish day schools, they are

often not very biblically literate. On the contrary, many embrace a secular humanistic philosophy.

My dear Aunt Maisie was a strong Jewish believer and a pioneer in Jewish ministry. She was a missionary to the Jews in South Africa for over thirty-five years. One day a Jewish man called her and questioned the validity of the Bible as the Word of God. He asked Maisie, "You don't really believe that a whale literally swallowed Jonah, do you?"

She answered matter-of-factly, like a mother instructing her child, "My dear young man, if the Bible said that *Jonah swallowed the whale*, I would believe it!"

Her answer may have seemed like a slap in the face to this intelligent young Jewish man. But it might also have served to shock him into the reality that as Jews we should believe that the whole Bible is the infallible and inspired Word of God. Maisie accepted whatever the Bible said, whether or not it made sense to human reasoning.

Sadly, this is not the case with many Jews. There are multitudes who believe that the Bible is merely a collection of the writings of men, or at best, historical stories. As with all people, there are Jewish skeptics, agnostics, and atheists.

Our response to skepticism among the Jewish people should not be to enter into endless debates with them but to counteract their unbelief with our faith. In the end, the strength of your conviction will win them over, not how persuasive you can be. So respond to their unbelief with an unwavering conviction and trust in the truth of God's Word. After all, we are called to win souls, not arguments. Sincere Jewish seekers can be won to the Lord when Christians share the gospel with a meek and humble spirit through the perspective of Old Testament prophecies.

Misconception #2. Jewish People Have a Clear Understanding of Heaven and Hell

Judaism does not present a clear view of the afterlife. Most Jews do not hold a solid belief in heaven for the redeemed and hell for the wicked, as Christianity teaches. Many believe that it is inhumane to think that a loving God would send people to hell forever. To them, the threat of hell for Jews who don't believe in Jesus is, at best, a scare tactic to try to convert them; at worst, it is anti-Semitic.

Some Jews think that Christians believe they are going to hell simply because they are Jews. But people don't go to hell because they are Jewish or because they are Gentile. We will all be condemned to eternity without God if we reject Jesus' atoning death on the cross, because only his sacrifice can take care of our sin problem. "There is no other name under heaven given among men by which we must be saved" (Acts 4:12).

I will explain how the enemy uses this subtle tactic of the enemy to keep Jews from believing in Jesus. Actually it is a "trick question" he uses to silence Christians from sharing Jesus with Jewish people. So, here is the question, you might have heard it before. Jewish people will often ask, "Are you saying that if Jews don't believe in Jesus they are going to hell?" The question is a valid one and the simple Biblical answer would be, yes, it's true. But here is the problem with the subtlety of the enemy in the question.

What is implied in this question though not clearly stated, is that Jews are going to hell *because they are Jews* and that becomes the issue. This therefore makes all Christians who share the gospel with the Jews look anti Semitic, but nothing could be further from the truth. The problem is that it is the wrong question which is loaded with guilt and untruth. So my answer is simply this:-

"This is the wrong question, the correct question is this. Can anyone go to heaven without believing in Jesus? The simple answer is, no, they cannot. No one can go to heaven except through Jesus (John 4:16). Jesus Himself stated this to the Jews. In fact, there are more Gentiles going to hell than Jews, simply because there are more Gentiles in the world." So, it is ok to gently rephrase the question so that all anti Semitic insinuations are taken out of the equation. Because the question has nothing to do with the person being Jewish or not being Jewish but rather about rejecting the only atoning sacrifice that God has made available to mankind, beginning with the Jewish people.

Misconception #3. Most Jewish People Have a Biblical Worldview.

Evangelical Christians tend to have conservative views on matters such as abortion on demand and same-sex marriage, based on Scripture. Since the whole Bible was written by Jews, they expect Jewish people to share their values. But many Jews are on the far left on these issues. With the exception of the very orthodox, Jews usually don't believe that the Bible is literally the inspired Word of God. They tend to see the Old Testament as an account of Jewish history (and they don't accept the New Testament at all), so it is not their frame of reference for normal, everyday life decisions.

Many Christians tend to withdraw from their Jewish friends when they realize they don't share the same biblical values. But our love and support for them should not be based on their sharing our worldview.

Misconception #4. All Jewish People View the Land of Israel from a Biblical Perspective

According to the Bible, the whole land of Israel is promised to the Jews by God (Genesis 15:17–21). However, they don't currently possess all of the territory promised to them in Scripture.

The Jewish people are constantly being told by the United Nations and its member states to give up land in exchange for peace. (Personally, I do not believe that compromise in this area would bring about peace anyway.)

Many Christians who support and love Israel are vocally opposed to having a Jewish state for Jews and a Palestinian state for Palestinians (what the media refers to as the "two-state solution"), because they don't see that in Scripture. Believing that they are standing with the Jewish people on this issue, they are shocked to discover that some Jews consider their apparently dogmatic views as an obstacle to peace.

Many Western Jews of the post-WWII generation are very critical of Israel and her policies, and some are not even supportive of the Jewish state. This is largely because most of them have never experienced anti-Semitism, and the Holocaust is just a part of history to them. They forget that the reason the State of Israel was formed was to protect and provide a safe haven for Jews everywhere.

We are to unconditionally love Jewish people, even if they don't agree with our biblical worldview when it comes to their land. The Bible says, "God demonstrates His own love toward us, in that while we were yet sinners, Messiah died for us" (Romans 5:8 TLV). Jesus loved us long before we had a biblical worldview. So let us go and do likewise.

TIPS FOR WITNESSING TO JEWISH PEOPLE

Use the Term "Messiah" Instead of "Christ"

Many Christians know that *Christ* is the Greek word for "anointed One," or Messiah. But the average Jewish person does not know this. To them, the term "Jesus Christ" is simply Christian jargon. Many think that Christ is merely Jesus' last name, rather than seeing this term as a proclamation that Jesus is the Messiah.

All Jews, regardless of their religious affiliation or where they stand with the Lord, can relate to the term *Messiah* to some degree. Most are still waiting for the Messiah to come and deliver Israel from her enemies and set up his kingdom from Jerusalem. Referring to Jesus as the Messiah instead of Christ, as Christians are accustomed to doing, provides common ground for connecting with Jewish people. It can open the door to witnessing to them if you ask who they believe the Messiah is, or what they think he will be.

One day I preached on Passover in a church where several Jewish guests had come out of curiosity when they heard I was speaking. After the service, a Christian who attended that church came up to me and said he had been witnessing to a Jewish friend of his for about three years but felt he was getting nowhere. He asked what was the best one-liner I could suggest he use. I thought for a moment, then said, "Tell him, 'Thank you for giving us *your promised Jewish Messiah.'*"

The next time I saw this man, I asked if he had used that phrase. He said he had. "And boy, did I get a reaction! His jaw dropped open, and then we entered into a three-hour discussion about the Messiah." By referring to Jesus as the Jewish Messiah, he contextualized the gospel.

Christians have unintentionally decontextualized the gospel in most of today's preaching and teaching, so the Jews have no clue that we are talking about a Jewish Messiah who came to Israel two thousand years ago. Contextualizing the gospel can mean the difference between heaven and hell for a lost Jewish soul who needs the Messiah.

Don't Dominate the Conversation

Jewish people usually expect evangelical Christians to be pushy and dogmatic in their approach. So surprise them by doing more listening than talking. You can guide the conversation without coming across as controlling. Ask questions more and make statements less.

For example, you could encourage them to read Psalm 22 or Isaiah 53 for themselves or ask them to read the prophecies in your presence—out loud if they are comfortable with it. Then ask questions like "Who do you think this is referring to?" or "What stands out to you in this passage of Scripture?" As you use this approach, showing respect for your Jewish friends and their decision-making ability and integrity, they will lead themselves to the Lord, which is the ideal situation. That way they'll feel they have come to the conclusion on their own rather than feeling pressured or manipulated to do so.

Don't Go Off on Rabbit Trails

Agnostics, skeptics, and intellectuals—whether Jews or not—will bring up all kinds of peripheral issues that will sidetrack you from sharing the gospel with them. Here are two of the main ones that I have been confronted with.

1. *What about aliens?* "Is it not vanity to think we are the only intelligent species in the whole universe and that everything revolves around us and our problems?" My response to this is "Maybe there is intelligent life on other planets. And if so, I'm sure God has a plan for them too. But right now, we are dealing for God's plan for human beings on Earth."

Though I am not personally convinced that aliens exist, this response averts the conversation from being sidetracked from the real issue, which is our sin problem. If I immediately shoot down this person's belief (or potential belief) in aliens, that will put up a wall between us. Instead I gently diffuse the situation to bring it back to the sin issue that we as humans deal with, and how only Jesus can take care of that.

2. *What about evolution?* This is often the biggest rebuttal to the gospel. Unbelievers often love to talk about dinosaurs roaming the earth before humans and how we all evolved from monkeys. I do not allow myself to get dragged into lengthy discussions over evolution versus creation. I simply explain that Jesus died for our sins, and specifically for theirs, to give us peace and eternal life.

I'm not saying there isn't a time and a place for debates on creationism versus evolution. After all, Paul the apostle used debates at times to win unbelieving Jews and Gentiles to the Lord. But there is a fine line between debating and coming across as argumentative and contentious. We should always be ready to give an answer to those who ask us hard questions, with a meek and gentle spirit. But keep in mind, it is almost impossible to convince people about the things of the Spirit of God if they do not have the Holy Spirit living inside them.

In the end, you cannot win people to Jesus by appealing to the mind. You need to appeal to the heart, to what they know deep within to be true. Ultimately, we need to bear in mind that the gospel was never meant to be a debate but rather a proclamation of God's truth!

Once an individual receives the Holy Spirit, it suddenly becomes clear that we were created by God in his image and likeness. But you cannot convince the natural man of this. The Bible says that spiritual things are spiritually discerned and that "the natural man does not receive the things of the Spirit of God" (1 Corinthians 2:14). So why waste time using natural reasoning to try to get a spiritual result?

THREE PRINCIPLES THAT LEAD TO GUARANTEED RESULTS

Following are three biblical principles for witnessing to Jewish people that have been proven over thirty years of experience in my own life and ministry. I have lost track of how many Jewish people I've led to the Lord following these principles. Of course, I learned them through years of trial and error, and

I'm still in the process of fine-tuning my application of them. But they have proven to be very effective for me, and the fruit has never stopped. I'm not saying that every time you use these three principles you will lead a Jewish person to the Lord. But if you apply them consistently, you will get results sooner or later.

Principle #1. Original Sin

This principle is foundational to the Christian faith and the story of redemption. But very few Jewish people have the same understanding of original sin that Christians do.

Since most Jews do not believe in the New Testament, we can bring our Jewish friends to the point of realizing that everyone has sinned (Romans 3:9) by using Old Testament Scriptures. The most obvious example is the account of the entry of sin through Adam and Eve in the garden of Eden (Genesis 3:1–13).

Also, in Psalm 51:5 (NIV), David says, "Surely I was sinful at birth, sinful from the time my mother conceived me." The NIV is the best translation to demonstrate this point, as most others say something like "In sin my mother conceived me" (NKJV), which many rabbis teach refers to King David acknowledging that he was conceived out of wedlock. David was not born out of wedlock, but some Orthodox Jews believe that he was an illegitimate son, and they use this Scripture to "prove" that point. They also claim that this explains why David's father, Jesse, did not bring him to see Nathan the prophet when Nathan asked him to bring all of his sons to determine which one would be anointed as king (1 Samuel 16:10–12).

While I was copastoring a congregation in California, the pastor told me about a Jewish guy (whom I'll call David) who had been in a severe accident. A huge truck had lost control, careened across the highway, and fell directly on the full length of his car, crushing it completely. David was not wearing a seatbelt. Yet he came out of the incident unharmed. The doctors couldn't figure out how he survived.

When I visited David, he showed me a photo of his car. The vehicle was so mangled, I was amazed he'd survived, let alone come out totally unscathed. He told me the guy who owned the junkyard it was towed to said he had never seen a car this badly crushed where the person had not been killed.

As I looked at this photo, I noticed something strange. Over the driver's seat, by the steering wheel, was something that looked like a bubble. It was as if an invisible, supernatural being had stood over the driver's section of the car and held it up to prevent it from being crushed by the truck.

If David had been wearing a seat belt, he would have been killed instantly. Since he wasn't, he naturally would have been thrown through the windshield. Instead, the impact shoved him into a small area between the steering wheel and the window.

Though David was not a religious person by nature, he knew God had spared him for a reason, as he had no explanation for this obvious miracle. But he wanted to know why God had saved his life. His rabbi could not give him a satisfactory answer, so he contacted a pastor—one who happened to know me. Since David was Jewish, the pastor referred him to me.

I met David in a parking lot because he didn't feel comfortable being seen talking to a Jewish believer. After he told me his amazing story, he asked me why God had saved him.

This happened early in my ministry, and I had not yet developed subtlety and wisdom. So I answered matter-of-factly that I knew exactly why God had spared him: so he could get saved from his sin, know Jesus as his Messiah, and go to heaven instead of hell. While this certainly was the truth, my approach could have been a bit more discreet.

David told me he was a good person and had lived a moral and upright life; therefore, he didn't believe he was a sinner. Because of this, no matter how much I shared with him about sin and redemption, no matter how many messianic prophecies I shared with him, I felt as if there was an invisible barrier I could not break through. Clearly, I was not gaining any ground as far as letting him know his life's purpose: to have a relationship with the living God through the promised Messiah of Israel.

We parted ways peacefully and agreed to meet again to discuss this further. A few days later I received a phone call saying that David was in the emergency room after suffering an almost fatal heart attack. Doctors told him he was suffering from chronic angina. Apart from a miracle, he would not survive due to complications and permanent damage to his heart.

I rushed to the ER to see him, along with a pastor friend of mine. To be honest, I hate hospitals. I know they help people, but I find them depressing because they are filled with sick and suffering people. David was no exception. He was hooked up to all kinds of pipes and drips and a heart-monitoring apparatus.

When I walked into David's room, he looked at me. Even with the oxygen mask over his face, I could see his expression, which looked like a combination of excitement and dread at my appearing.

I wanted to help this man. But I felt powerless to do so. The Devil whispered to me that I was wasting my time and I should just let David die in peace without bothering him with talk of salvation and eternity. But I knew I'd been sent there by God. This man was literally on the brink of eternity. Heaven and hell stood before him, and in a matter of days he would go to one or the other.

But what could I say? David was a brilliant Jewish man, with the IQ of a genius and more degrees than a thermometer. He had six master's degrees and a few PHDs. But when I opened my mouth, all I could talk about was what I'd already gone over with David repeatedly: that he was a sinner and needed forgiveness from a Savior. I urged him to make his peace with God before he faced eternity.

My attempt felt rather pathetic. But the Holy Spirit would not let me talk about anything except the fact of original sin and that we are all sinners.

Even in his near-death state, David stuck to his claim that he was a good person. Clearly, I was getting nowhere and gaining no ground. The Enemy kept telling me I was ruthless and merciless, and that I should leave this dying man alone. But I knew in my heart I had to obey the Holy Spirit.

As I continued to share, I thought about the kind of life David had lived. Everyone who knew him said he was a great guy, a moral and caring person who helped people in need whenever he could. All of a sudden the Holy Spirit said to me, "Tell him you agree with him that he is a good person." Though I knew the Holy Spirit was speaking to me, this made no sense. Surely God would never give me an instruction that contradicted Scripture. Nevertheless, I recognized his gentle voice and immediately obeyed.

"David," I said, "I know you are a good person."

He looked so shocked that I was finally agreeing with him, I was afraid he might have another heart attack right then and there.

I continued. "I'm sure you are a better person than I am. But even good people have done bad things."

He looked confused.

"I know you've never murdered anyone. But have you ever hated someone so much that you *wanted* to kill him? I know you've never committed adultery. But did you ever look at a woman in a lustful way?" I did not tell him I was using the New Testament as my basis for this. But the Word of God will never return void when we use it (Isaiah 55:11), whether a person is a believer or not.

"David," I said, "you can sin in your heart without committing a blatant act of wrongdoing. And in God's eyes, you have sinned."

He offered no response. David looked so exhausted, I wondered if he wanted to argue but didn't have the energy or strength to do so.

The Lord gently told me, *You have obeyed. You can go now.*

It was scary for me to leave David without leading him in a prayer of salvation. As I exited his room, my mind went crazy with all kinds of questions and accusations. *What if he dies without you leading him to the Lord? You are so useless! You don't know what you're doing. You're wasting your time and his. Can't you finish the job you started?*

I am an evangelist to the core. I have been from the day I was saved. I'd already led hundreds, maybe thousands to the Lord. But I knew I had heard God's voice telling me to leave David alone now. Though this man's eternity hung in the balance, I needed to obey. God knew best and he had a plan.

As I left the hospital, I prayed for David to be at peace.

A few days later I heard that David was well enough to be transferred to the part of the hospital for patients without life-threatening conditions. His heart was still in bad shape, but for now he was stable.

I also heard that his nephew Bob, a Jewish pharmacist, had been saved a few weeks earlier, and he was really on fire, witnessing to everyone. He visited David in the hospital and asked him point blank, "Hey, Uncle David, are you saved?"

Now, that breaks all the rules of Jewish evangelism, using Christian clichés that make no sense to the average Jew. But David answered, "Actually, I didn't think I needed to be saved. Until a Jewish messianic rabbi named Geoffrey Cohen shared with me in the ER the other day. Now I think I do need to be saved."

Though shocked that Jewish evangelism could be so easy, Bob replied, "Okay, then, do you want to pray to receive Jesus right now?"

David responded, "I would love to!"

Bob led his uncle in the sinner's prayer to receive Jesus as his Lord and Messiah. David's face glowed with peace. The two men hugged and cried and were filled with joy.

David was a brilliant and well-educated Jew, but he had to be convinced he was a sinner before he would let anyone talk to him about his need to receive Jesus. I had shared messianic prophecies with him, but that was premature. Even if he believed Jesus was the Messiah, he did not see that as relevant to his life. But once David realized that he had sinned, even though he was a "good guy" in human terms, it was easy for his nephew—who knew little of how to appropriately witness to a Jew—to lead his uncle to the Lord. As Scripture says, one sows, another waters, but God brings the increase (see 1 Corinthians 3:6).

Even when dealing with the most brilliant and educated of Jews, it is the fundamentals of the gospel that bring a Jew (or any person) to faith.

David lived only a few weeks after receiving Yeshua as his Messiah. But I had such sweet fellowship with him during that time, I tear up just thinking about it. Over and over, he asked me to read to him from the book of Revelation, especially about the twelve pearly gates in the New Jerusalem that represent each of the twelve tribes of Israel (he'd always had a fascination with pearls) and the streets of pure gold that he would be walking on soon. I have never seen anyone so eager to get to heaven as soon as possible. I look forward to seeing him there one day, when we can stand at those gates together and discuss the wonders of God!

Principle #2. The Need for Blood Atonement
Though many Christians are unaware of this, there is a huge difference between biblical Judaism as presented in the Old

Testament and modern-day Judaism. Biblical Judaism centered around the feasts and regular animal blood sacrifices, which were administered by the Levitical priesthood on behalf of the people. One of the foundations of biblical Judaism is that there is no forgiveness without a blood sacrifice.

This practice was established in the Torah (the first five books of Moses). Leviticus 17:11 says, "The life of the flesh is in the blood, and I have given it to you upon the altar to make atonement for your souls; for it is the blood that makes atonement for the soul."

Biblical Judaism was practiced until AD 72, when the second temple was destroyed by the Romans and the Jews were scattered into the Diaspora (the nations). That situation presented a dilemma. Worship had been focused around the temple in Jerusalem and blood atonement through the animal sacrificial system, which was all administered through the Levitical priesthood. But now there was no longer a temple. So Judaism had to be redefined.

Today, rabbinical Judaism has replaced biblical Judaism. Here are the main distinctions between the original Jewish faith and the modern-day version:

- The Levitical priesthood was replaced by what we know today as rabbis. They run or lead the synagogues. Under the biblical system, a male had to be a direct descendant of Aaron and belong to the tribe of Levi in order to minister as a priest. Now any Jew who studies in a Yeshiva (Jewish Bible school) can receive his credentials as a rabbi, regardless of what tribe he descends from.

- After the Jews were exiled from their homeland, the destroyed temple was replaced by the synagogue as the center of worship, and the system of blood sacrifice was abolished.

- The Talmud became the main source of interpreting the Torah. The Talmud is essentially the ancient rabbis' interpretation and explanation of the Torah. The Prophets were looked upon as being good to study (and still are).

But since the coming of Jesus, their importance has been minimized. Because so many prophecies are of a messianic nature and seem to point strongly to Yeshua, the Jewish leadership faced a choice. Accept that the prophecies clearly point to Jesus as Messiah and officially tell the Jewish nation that they were wrong to reject Him. Or reinterpret the prophecies, claiming that they were not messianic in nature. They chose the latter. This is why prophetic chapters such as Isaiah 53 and Daniel 9 are still controversial in Jewish circles. Messianic Jews say they speak of the Messiah, as do Christians, while the rabbis and other Jewish leaders say they do not.

- Modern-day Judaism essentially says that Teshuvah (repentance), Mitzvoth (good deeds), and prayer have replaced the need for a blood sacrifice. But therein lies a problem. What the rabbis say in the Talmud concerning the requirement of substitutionary blood atonement for sin, and what the Word of God (the Torah) says, contradict each other.

If what the rabbis and ancient Talmudic writers say clearly contradicts what Moses said in the Torah, I have to go with the Torah.

For example, Moses said that without a blood sacrifice there is no forgiveness of sin (Leviticus 17:11). But where is our atonement today? God's Law does not change just because circumstances change, and his demand for an innocent blood sacrifice for the guilty sinner remains. Just because the temple was destroyed by the Romans, that does not change God's principles or pave the way for a new belief system to replace the foundational requirement of a blood sacrifice to atone for sin.

Principle #3. The Messiahship of Jesus

Once we have established that we are all born in sin and that only a blood sacrifice can satisfy God's wrath and judgment, we have to provide a viable answer to this serious problem. Then we have to explain that the blood of bulls and goats, as prescribed under the old covenant, was not enough to wash away our sins; it only covered them. True atonement required a far better sacrifice: that of a person who had never sinned, who lived a perfect life. This is what the ancient prophets spoke about. The old covenant was not adequate to meet this need. This leads us to our next key point: that these requirements were only fulfilled through Jesus and his sacrifice on the cross. That is why God made a new covenant with Israel.

Jesus is the solution to our sin problem. Not one of many possible solutions, but the only solution. He is the only one who could possibly fulfill all of the Old Testament prophecies. He has already fulfilled every Old Testament prophecies concerning the first coming of the Messiah, and he will someday fulfill those that concern the second coming. Therefore, we have to establish the messiahship of Jesus in the minds of Jews who are not yet believers.

Isaiah 53 is arguably the most controversial of the prophecies in Jewish circles. In this chapter, we see a graphic portrayal of what is now referred to as "The Suffering Servant," bearing the sins of God's people. It talks of him being "despised and rejected," someone from whom men hid their faces (v. 3). It goes on to say that he "shall bear their iniquities" (v. 11), then that he "bore the sin of many" (v. 12), and "by his stripes we are healed" (v. 5). Isaiah also says, "For the transgressions of My people He was stricken" (v. 8). When Isaiah made those statements, he was referring to the Messiah paying the price for the transgressions of his fellow Israelites.

As believers, we realize that this now-famous chapter is a description of Jesus. But most Jews, especially those in biblically literate circles, need further convincing.

Many believe that Isaiah 53 describes Israel, not the Messiah. But where it says, "For the transgressions of my people He was stricken," how can that be speaking of Israel? Israel cannot bear their own iniquities.

Some Jewish people claim that Isaiah's description would fit any Jew who has been through the Holocaust. But as horrible as the Holocaust was, no Jew could atone for his or her own sins or the sins of his or her people through suffering, no matter how severe that suffering might be. Only someone who was spotless and without sin or blemish could atone for our sins. This leaves only one option according to the prophecies: Yeshua.

Because of the controversial nature of Isaiah 53 as a messianic prophecy, I usually avoid using it when witnessing to Jewish people. Instead, I focus on these messianic prophecies:

MESSIAH HAD TO BE CRUCIFIED

I usually begin my witnessing to Jewish people by having them read Psalm 22. Then I ask what or who they think this passage is talking about. Since they won't have any preprogrammed objections (as they do with Isaiah 53), they are more likely to take it at face value. In addition, in my opinion, Psalm 22 paints a clearer picture of the gospel than any other prophecy in Scripture.

The first time I read Psalm 22, I was in the army in South Africa and going through a rough time during boot camp. A Christian had been witnessing to me, and one day he gave me Psalm 22 to read. By the time I got to verse 18, I thought he had given me a portion of the New Testament. In frustration, I gave it back to him and told him in no uncertain terms that Jews do not believe in the New Testament. To my shock and amazement, he told me it was from the Old Testament, and that it was written by one of the heroes of the Jewish faith, King David himself. I looked at the introduction to Psalm 22 to confirm his words, and sure enough, it said it was a Psalm of David.

I had no idea what to do with this. So I decided to research the original Hebrew version of this passage. I figured the one my friend gave me must be a bad translation done by Gentiles who didn't know the Hebrew language. But to my surprise, the official Jewish interpretation as written by the Hebrew scholars was very similar.

The only major difference was in verse 16, where it says, "They pierced My hands and My feet." The Jewish translation said, "Like a lion his hands and feet." That seemed a rather odd wording, because it made no grammatical sense at all.

As I studied further, I found that this phrase could be translated either "Like a lion" or "They pierced," depending on the original manuscript used.

With more research, I found out that in the earliest manuscripts available—such as the Dead Sea scrolls, which date back to more than one hundred years before Jesus—the Hebrew word used in that verse was even more graphic. It means "to gouge" or "to bore through." "They pierced" seems to allude to a minor pinprick that draws blood, such as when people have their ears pierced. "To gouge" or "to bore through" is a much better description of what happens when a grown man is secured to a cross with thick, one-foot-long nails. Clearly God gave us an amazingly accurate and detailed picture of Jesus at the crucifixion.

But that presented a big problem for me. If either translation could be correct in the original Hebrew, why did the rabbis and Hebrew scholars choose "like a lion" over "they pierced"—especially since that wording doesn't make grammatical sense? Were they trying to hide something? Did "they pierced" sound too much like Jesus, especially since the rest of the Psalm seems to clearly describe someone being crucified?

God used Psalm 22 to plant a seed in my heart that Jesus probably was the Messiah. That seed grew until I finally gave my heart to Jesus about three years later. I can't tell you how many Jews I have led to the Lord using Psalm 22—including my Orthodox Jewish grandmother.

The amazing thing about Psalm 22 is that it was written by King David more than eight hundred years before crucifixion was even invented by the Romans. Yet David describes with disarming accuracy almost every medical symptom suffered by a person who is being crucified. For example, verse 14 says, "All My bones are out of joint." This happens because the weight of the person hanging on a cross for so long eventually pulls the bones out of his sockets. In an effort to breathe, the person tries to hoist up the weight of his body using his feet. Roman soldiers often broke the legs of a person being crucified so he could no longer do this and thus would die sooner.

Guards broke the legs of the two people who were crucified on either side of Jesus, but when they came to him, they discovered he was already dead (John 19:36). This specific detail fulfilled the Old Testament prophecy in Exodus 12:46 that said, "Not one of His bones shall be broken." The lamb sacrificed on Passover was not to have any broken bones. John the Baptist referred to Jesus as the Lamb of God who takes away the sin of the world (John 1:29). Not coincidentally, Jesus was crucified on Passover.

Verse 18 of Psalm 22 prophesied that soldiers would divide up the Messiah's garments among them and cast lots for his clothing at his crucifixion. This prophecy was fulfilled because the soldiers did not want to break Jesus' beautiful seamless robe, so they cast lots to decide who would wear it. I sometimes wonder whether the Roman soldier who wore it ended up getting saved because of the strong anointing that would be on anything Jesus touched.

Jesus fulfilled many other specific prophecies. But for most Jewish people, it is more effective to focus on one or two of the most obvious ones, like Psalm 22, and encourage them to respond to what they just read, rather than to use some of the prophecies that could have dual interpretation or are controversial in Jewish circles, like Isaiah 53.

MESSIAH HAD TO BE BORN OF A VIRGIN

Hundreds of years before Jesus was born, Isaiah prophesied that Messiah would be born to a virgin. Of course, this would be the only time in history that would happen, because it is physically impossible for a woman to conceive without the seed of a man. But this crucial sign came to pass with the birth of Jesus, as the gospel records in Matthew 1:23, "'The virgin shall be with child, and bear a son, and they shall call his name Immanuel,' which is translated, 'God with us.'"

This passage refers back to the prophecy in Isaiah 7:14 that says, "The Lord Himself will give you a sign: Behold, the virgin shall conceive and bear a Son, and shall call His name Immanuel."

The Hebrew word translated "virgin" in the English is *almah*, which many rabbis argue would be more accurately translated "young maiden," thus debunking the Christian claim of the virgin birth. While that perspective makes sense from a contemporary perspective, we must take into account the cultural context of this passage. In the time Isaiah wrote this prophecy, "young maiden" referred to a young unmarried woman. In that culture, premarital sex was punishable by death and virginity prior to marriage was a virtue to be cherished. A young single woman was assumed to be a virgin. Therefore, the terms may be used interchangeably. In fact, the Hebrew word *betulah* is used fifty times in the Bible, and in thirty-one of those cases, the NJPSV translates it as "maiden."[11]

The rabbis claim that Christians changed the translation from "young maiden" to "virgin" a few hundred years after Jesus came

---

[11]Dr. Michael Brown, *Answering Jewish Objections to Jesus*, vol. 3 (Michigan: Baker Books, 2003), 21.

into the world. However, this is not factual. The Old Testament was translated into Greek about two hundred years before Jesus was born so the Jews living in the Diaspora could have the Bible in their own language. (This was called the Septuagint.) And those Hebrew scholars used the Greek word for "virgin" in this verse.

Could it be the rabbis argue so strongly against the virgin birth because the early Jewish scholars' translation leaves only one option: proof that Jesus is the Messiah?

MESSIAH HAD TO BE BORN IN BETHLEHEM AND COME FROM THE TRIBE OF JUDAH

Micah 5:2 says, "But you, Bethlehem Ephrathah, though you are little among the thousands of Judah, yet out of you shall come forth to Me the One to be Ruler in Israel, whose goings forth are from of old, from everlasting."

Only God has no beginning, so this prophecy clearly points to Messiah's deity, which is something mainstream Jewry does not believe in.

This passage also indicates where Messiah would be born (Bethlehem) and the tribe he would belong to (Judah). Both of these details point specifically to Jesus.

The name of the city Jesus was born in foreshadowed who he would prove to be. In the original Hebrew, *Beth* means "house," and *lechem* means "bread." So, Jesus was born in the "House of Bread." In John 6:51 (NIV), Jesus referred to himself as "the living bread that came down from heaven." Then he said, "If anyone eats of this bread, he will live forever." This saying created no small amount of consternation among the disciples, and even caused some to stop following him.

MESSIAH WOULD BE RAISED FROM THE DEAD

Psalm 16:10–11 says, "You will not leave my soul in Sheol, nor will You allow Your Holy One to see corruption. You will show me the path of life; in Your presence is fullness of joy; at your right hand are pleasures forevermore."

Here, "Your Holy One" is a messianic term, and this passage says that he will never see decay. All of mankind is subject to the curse of death and decay, ever since sin entered the world though Adam and Eve. But Jesus broke that curse. His body never decayed or rotted because he rose from the dead after three days. This proved that he was the Messiah, who forever destroyed sin and death. Because of his sinless life, his death on the cross, and his subsequent resurrection, all who believe in him will never have to suffer the sting of sin and death. Hallelujah!

Psalm 110:1–2 says, "The Lord said to my Lord, 'Sit at My right hand, till I make Your enemies Your footstool.' The Lord shall send the rod of Your strength out of Zion. Rule in the midst of Your enemies!"

This psalm of David builds a case not only for the resurrection, but also for the deity of Messiah. No man has ever sat at the right hand of the Father or ever will. That spot is reserved for the Messiah alone.

MESSIAH HAD TO COME BEFORE THE DESTRUCTION OF THE SECOND TEMPLE

Daniel 9:25–26 says:

> Know therefore and understand, that from the going forth of the command to restore and build Jerusalem until Messiah the Prince, there shall be seven weeks and sixty-two weeks; the street shall be built again, and the wall, even in troublesome times. And after the sixty-two weeks Messiah shall be cut off, but not for Himself; and the people of the prince who is to come shall destroy the city and the sanctuary. The end of it shall be with a flood, and till the end of the war desolations are determined.

Daniel prophesied that "the prince who is to come shall destroy the city and the sanctuary." This spoke of Titus, the Roman general who destroyed the Jewish temple in AD 72. But the controversial part in Jewish circles is that verse 26 says the Messiah will be "cut off" (in other words, die) *before* the temple is destroyed. Yeshua was indeed crucified before this event happened.

So, the Jewish leaders were again faced with a decision. Either acknowledge that this passage could only point to Jesus or discount the clear implication of the prophecy. They chose to say that the original Hebrew word Moshiach did not refer to the Messiah but rather to "an anointed one." (Even if this were the case, the term "Anointed One" in Hebrew is known to be a messianic term, so their argument has no teeth.)

MESSIAH WOULD BE BOTH GOD AND MAN

Isaiah 9:6–7, part of the Hebrew Scriptures, states this in no uncertain terms. "For unto us a Child is born, unto us a Son is given; and the government will be upon His shoulder. And His name will be called Wonderful, Counselor, Mighty God, Everlasting Father, Prince of Peace. Of the increase of His government and peace there will be no end, upon the throne of David and over His kingdom, to order it and establish it with judgment and justice from that time forward, even forever. The zeal of the Lord of hosts will perform this."

Some great human leaders may be called "wonderful" or "counselor." But there are two names on this list that no mere mortal could ever bear: "Mighty God" and "Everlasting Father." Clearly this refers to a man born from a woman, as it says, "Unto us a Child is born, unto us a Son is given." However, "of the increase of His government and peace there will be no end" clearly refers to a Messiah who has no end to his life and who will rule over Israel forever. This individual would have to be both God and man at the same time. This leaves only one option: Yeshua, the Messiah, who is both 100 percent God and 100 percent man at the same time.

Isaiah was looking into the future when he wrote this more than seven hundred years before Jesus was born. He was clearly speaking of the Messiah, who has come and is yet to come, who will rule and reign forever.

This prophecy also proves that Messiah will be called the Son of God, which many Jews say is impossible, even blasphemous. But it's right here in the Old Testament. Even though modern-day Judaism denies that God can have a son, the Hebrew Scriptures clearly prophesy that this is the case.

The Old Testament is pregnant with such infallible proofs pointing to Jesus as Messiah. The prophecies I've mentioned here are by no means an exhaustive list, nor are they intended to be. But they are enough to convince a sincere seeker, whether Jewish or not, that Jesus is indeed the promised Messiah of Israel. There are many books that give details of all the messianic prophecies. But I want to help you see that witnessing to a Jew is simple and manageable for the average Christian.

Remember, the goal is not to impress your Jewish friends with your knowledge or to win an argument, but to win a heart for Jesus. This should not become an intellectual exercise or a battle between your mind and someone else's. That is based on pride, not love. However, if the person is sincerely questioning the Scripture and its context regarding the Messiah, take all the time needed to explain the various passages.

I have chosen what I believe to be the simplest and clearest prophecies that in my opinion build the most watertight case for Jesus. I have used these prophecies to lead countless Jews to the Lord over the last few decades, and I believe that you will be successful as well if you use them as the Spirit leads you.

Always bathe your witnessing in prayer and maintain a humble spirit. Above all, let your heart be filled with love, because in the end, it's the love of God that wins people's hearts. With wisdom, love, and much prayer, you can use Old Testament prophecies to win your Jewish neighbors and friends to the Lord.

SHARE YOUR TESTIMONY

Never underestimate the power of your personal story of how you came to the Lord. A Jewish person can argue with you doctrinally, but no one can dispute the testimony of a transformed life. Your story will show that even Gentiles are not Christians by birth—they have to come into a personal relationship with God by their own choice of receiving Jesus into their hearts. This will speak volumes to your Jewish friends, because most Jews assume that a Christian is someone who is born of Christian parents. They have no idea that Gentiles have to decide to *become* Christians.

Your testimony will force them to rethink this paradigm that anyone is born a Christian. Once they grasp this truth, their lives will change for eternity.

ANSWER QUESTIONS AND OBJECTIONS

After one of our messianic services at Gateway's North Richland Hills campus, I met a Jewish man (whom I'll call Nathan). He was very orthodox and belonged to a Lubavitch synagogue a few hours away. He told me that after his divorce, he met a beautiful Christian girl. Though he never would have imagined dating a Christian, they started seeing each other and he quickly fell in love with her. She told him that although she liked him a lot, she could not seriously date someone who was not a believer, so the relationship could not advance any further. She did not want to be unequally yoked in marriage to an unbeliever (2 Corinthians 6:14).

Nathan loved her very much. But since he was a devout Jew, he could not embrace her faith in Jesus. This situation was painful for them both.

She suggested that he come with her to the monthly messianic service at Gateway, as she had heard about a Jewish pastor there who came from an orthodox background (me). She hoped that somehow I could help them bridge the gap.

After the service, Nathan stood in line to speak to me. He waited patiently for a long time, as I was praying for a lot of people and our services are very well attended. When his turn came, I greeted him warmly and shook his hand. The first thing he said to me was "Hi, I'm Nathan, and I'm Jewish. But I'm not a Christian."

I looked him in the eye and replied, "Great to meet you, Nathan. Neither am I." Of course, I am a strong believer in Jesus. But I call myself a messianic Jew. I avoid the term *Christian* because of centuries of Christian anti-Semitism and persecution of the Jews.

We talked briefly, and I learned that he was very orthodox and highly educated, holding a number of college degrees.

A couple of months later, my assistant, Carina, got an e-mail from Nathan saying he wanted to meet me. He lived almost five hours away, but he asked for at least two or three uninterrupted hours of my time.

My first thought was that he must be a deprogrammer sent by the Lubavitchers to try to bring me back to Orthodox Judaism. I had experience with that in Jerusalem years before, when I spent a few months in a Yeshiva with deprogrammers who boasted that they had brought more than twenty young Jewish believers back to Judaism. But after four months of hearing almost every possible Jewish objection to the gospel from some of the top rabbis in the land, I came out stronger in my faith than ever before. And more convinced than ever that Jesus is indeed the promised Messiah.

I would not recommend this path to any young Jewish believer, unless clearly directed by the Holy Spirit. That kind of intense deprogramming could have devastating consequences for anyone who is not very established in the Word. But I had been a believer for three and a half years before I did this. And even though I later obtained a bachelor's degree in theology, what I learned in Bible school paled in comparison to how much I grew through my experience in the Yeshiva.

Even though I thought Nathan might be a deprogrammer, that did not intimidate me. Instead, I saw it as an opportunity to share the gospel with him, regardless of his motives or agenda.

When Nathan arrived in my office, he sat down and said, "When I told you I was Jewish and not Christian, and you said, 'Neither am I,' my girlfriend and I were both confused. For most of our five-hour drive back, we discussed the meaning of what you said. I've been so curious about your statement that I couldn't take it anymore, so I had to come and talk to you about it."

After explaining to him why I avoided the term *Christian* when speaking to Jewish people, I shared in detail the story of how I came from an Orthodox Jewish background to discover Yeshua as the promised Messiah. He listened intently.

We went from there into a lengthy discussion with deep and probing questions, ranging from why the rabbis of today don't believe Jesus is the Messiah to analyzing the Old Testament prophecies. Nathan was so brilliant and mentally sharp, for the first hour I was convinced he was indeed a deprogrammer. But as we entered into the second hour, he saw that I had a logical answer for every question, and I began to think that maybe he was a sincere seeker after all.

Nathan was testing me, and he made no bones about it. He wanted to know if I was "for real," as he put it, and whether I really "knew my stuff." No one else had been able to answer his questions to his satisfaction. To win a man of this caliber and education, with a keen lawyer's mind, I would have to be unmovable. I was "on trial," so to speak, so I could show no weakness or chinks in my armor. I had to be unflinching and strong in my convictions if I was to win his heart over for the Lord.

After I responded to each question, Nathan asked politely, "Do you mind if I ask another question?" Eventually I told him, "You don't need to ask for my permission every time. There is no question you can ask that will intimidate me, so just go for it."

For nearly three hours, he presented almost every Jewish objection to the gospel that had ever been asked—at least if felt that way to me. I was mentally and spiritually exhausted. But I couldn't show it. This man's soul was at stake, and I had to remain strong to the end. Nathan would be a huge influence to the orthodox community in his city if he gave his heart to the Lord. Failure was not an option.

Finally, he actually ran out of questions. He looked me in the eye and said, "Clearly you are genuine, and your faith is genuine. You know what you believe and why you believe it."

I was thrilled! I sensed the Holy Spirit telling me I had passed the test and that Nathan was close to salvation. "Do you have any more questions?" I asked.

He pondered a moment, then said, "I can't think of any."

"So, is there anything preventing you from receiving Yeshua as your Messiah?"

"Not that I can think of."

Right then and there, I led him in a prayer to receive Yeshua as his Messiah. It was one of the most fulfilling moments of my life.

I love rising to the challenge of reaching out to people like Nathan, because nothing is too difficult for our God and nothing can stand in the light of the glorious gospel of our Messiah. All objections of man melt away in the presence of his love and his Word.

Many believers are too intimidated to let the brilliant minds of this world present all of their objections to the gospel. But we have no reason to be afraid. The gospel message can stand strong and proud in the marketplace of new ideas and every contemporary objection the world can throw at us.

Nathan came to me full of skepticism and objections to the gospel, but he left that day full of faith and the Holy Spirit. All of my sufferings and trials as a Jewish believer would be worth it even if just for this one precious soul!

Nathan went back to the synagogue he came from and told them he had found the Messiah. When they asked him who the Messiah was, and he said, "Yeshua," they were flabbergasted. Many lively debates ensued. And Nathan made a stand for the Lord in his community.

I'm sure many other people have discovered this simple yet effective method and have used it often without even realizing it. Certainly, Paul the apostle used it, because Scripture says he reasoned with the Jews and overcame all their objections, often with great results. Acts 17:2–5 (NIV) says:

> As was his custom, Paul went into the synagogue, and on three Sabbath days he reasoned with them from the Scriptures, explaining and proving that the Messiah had to suffer and rise from the dead. "This Jesus I am proclaiming to you is the Messiah," he said. Some of the Jews were persuaded and joined Paul and Silas, as did a large number of God-fearing Greeks and quite a few prominent women.

Paul won many Jews and Greeks to the Lord using this method, in many cities, usually in the synagogues, over and over again.

When dealing with those who are intellectually and philosophically minded, as were the Greeks in Paul's day, or those who have many objections to the gospel, as many Jews do today, it is sometimes necessary to answer every question they might have. In Paul's case, he spent three whole Sabbath days with them, which makes my mere three hours seem short in comparison. But as we deal with a world that has countless philosophies and worldviews that are contrary to the Scriptures, we need to be willing to spend time with people and answer all objections they may have. If we feel intimidated about responding to questions, we could lose the battle for our culture and our world. Many people are looking for something real and genuine that can answer the deepest needs of the human soul.

THE OPEN DOOR CIRCLE METHOD

I stumbled upon this method by accident about four years ago. I say that tongue-in-cheek, of course, as I believe nothing happens by chance when we are serving the Lord. But I found this to be incredibly effective the first time I tried it, so I've used it over and over. I would by no means dare to claim that this system is foolproof or a guaranteed method of leading Jewish people to the Lord, as in the end people have a free will and make their own choices. However, I have had a phenomenal success rate. In fact, over the last month alone, I have led three Jewish people to the Lord using this method.

Of course, it can be used to lead anyone to the Lord, not only Jewish people. This is mostly for witnessing to those who have numerous objections to the gospel, so it is an ideal method for skeptics, atheists, and agnostics of any background.

Here is how I initially "stumbled" upon it.

Shortly after I led Nathan to the Lord, I met another Jewish seeker who had a Christian girlfriend. Apparently, God was using pretty Gentile Christian women at Gateway as catalysts to lead Jewish men to the Lord! I met with them at an Italian restaurant, so we had about an hour to talk. I answered each of Peter's objections to the gospel, especially his questions about Jesus being the Messiah. As I spoke, I had a vision in the form of a word picture from the Lord. I saw a circle with about thirty open doors on the table between us. Each of the doors represented a Jewish objection to the gospel. As I answered each objection, a door closed. After about an hour of debate and discussion, all but one of the doors were closed. The final door that remained open led directly to Jesus. As I thought about this, I recalled John 10:1–6, where Jesus said that he is the door.

I asked Peter, as I had with Nathan, if he had any more questions. He said that he did not. I asked him if there was any reason for him not to receive Jesus as his Messiah. To my great joy, he answered that there was not, and he prayed then and there. As he prayed, an indescribable peace came over all three of us and tears ran down our cheeks. Although I did not get to see this seeker again after this prayer I trust that He who began the good work in him will perfect it as it states in Phillipians 1:6.

Words cannot describe how fulfilling this kind of ministry is. I have preached to crowds of hundreds and even thousands over the years, but nothing is as rewarding as spending time with the lost sheep of the house of Israel and seeing them come back to the God of their fathers. I never tire of these moments, and I savor them for years afterward.

I decided to call this the "open door circle method." Now, whenever I sit down opposite a sincere Jewish seeker, I visualize a circle on the table between us, and a door closing with every objection to the gospel I answer, until the only door left open is the one that leads to Jesus. At the end of our time together, after the last door closes, I offer an opportunity to receive Jesus as Messiah. I want to try to "seal the deal" while the anointing is present.

Proverbs 11:30 says that "he that wins souls is wise." It does not say that he who proves his point is wise. The desired conclusion is for a precious lost sheep of the house of Israel to find his or her Messiah.

You might be wondering, "How do I answer all of a Jewish person's questions, let alone get to the point where I can lead him or her to the Lord?" First, trust the Holy Spirit to give you wisdom in your answers, as he is your ultimate source and guide. But you also need practical knowledge to answer people's objections to Jesus.

Below is a list of the most common objections I have encountered over my twenty-nine years of Jewish ministry, with responses for each one. I struggled with these questions myself before I gave my heart to the Lord. This should cover the most common objections of the average Jewish person you might witness to. I'll make the answers short and to the point so you can easily become familiar with them.

Objection: If Jesus is the Messiah, why do the rabbis not believe in him?

Answer: The Jewish leadership in Moses' time didn't believe in him either. Many wanted to rebel against him. They also rejected almost all of the prophets, including Isaiah, Jeremiah, and Hosea. But that doesn't mean those men were not sent from God. Religious leaders aren't infallible, and sometimes they can lead people astray.

Objection: If Jesus is the Messiah, why don't most Jews believe in him?

Answer: A majority consensus is not necessarily an indication of truth. Besides, if you study the Old Testament, you will see that throughout history only a small Jewish remnant truly followed the God of Israel. In fact, in the days of Elijah the prophet, the majority of Jews were led astray by false idols and Baal worship.

At one point he thought that he was the only Jew left who was truly following the God of Israel.

Objection: I thought the Messiah was supposed to bring world peace. If Jesus is the Messiah, why is there not peace in the world?

Answer: You're right, the Messiah is supposed to bring world peace. And Jesus will … at his second coming. But first he wants to bring peace to your world and your heart. He wants people to choose him willingly before he returns as the ruling, reigning, conquering King.

Objection: We Jews don't need a middle man to get to God. We go to him directly. That is a Christian concept, not a Jewish one.

Answer: Actually, the Jewish people have always had a mediator between them and God. The Levitical priesthood made blood sacrifices to God on behalf of the people, and the high priest presented a sacrifice for the nation once a year on the Day of Atonement. We've also had great Jewish leaders mediate on our behalf with God, such as Moses, the judges, and the prophets. The concept of a mediator is definitely a Jewish and biblical concept.

Objection: Becoming a Christian would be a betrayal to my family and everything our forefathers fought and died for. I was born a Jew and I will die as a Jew!

Answer: God doesn't want you to become a Christian. He wants you to receive Yeshua (Jesus) as the promised Jewish Messiah and become a completed or fulfilled Jew through him. Yes, you were born a Jew, and you will die as a Jew in Messiah if you receive him, and then you will be with God forever.

Objection: Christians have killed Jews for centuries, and even forced them to convert on pain of death. How can I betray my people by willingly converting?

Answer: You are not changing religions; you are coming back to the God of your fathers through the Messiah. The people who killed and persecuted our fathers in the name of Christianity weren't truly Christians, because they practiced the exact opposite of what Jesus taught. Besides, if being faithful to the God of our fathers makes you look like a traitor in the eyes of some, then wear that name proudly. In the end, we all have to make a choice. Are we here to please God or man? There are times when it is impossible to please both.

Objection: The Christian concept of a blood sacrifice seems barbaric and primitive. As a twenty-first-century Jew, that doesn't seem necessary.

Answer: Actually, the necessity for a blood sacrifice is not a Christian concept, but a Jewish one. The sacrificial system in the Old Testament was the focal point of Jewish life and the only method for atonement in ancient Israel.

Objection: If the Christian religion comes out of Judaism, why do Christians keep the Sabbath on Sunday instead of Saturday, like we do?

Answer: Most Christian scholars agree that the original Sabbath is from sunset on Friday to sunset on Saturday (as the Jews observe). However, Sunday is the day Jesus rose from the dead (and has come to be known as the Lord's Day), so most Christians choose to worship then. But whatever day we keep the Sabbath, the most important thing is that we set aside at least one day a week to rest and focus on God.

Objection: Isn't it narrow-minded and arrogant to say that the Christian religion is the only way to heaven and that people from all other religions are going to hell?

Answer: First, embracing the Christian religion is not what gets you into heaven. It is receiving the person of Jesus into your heart. Second, none of us deserves to go to heaven. We should be thankful that God provided a way for any of us to be saved at all. And this gift is open to everyone, no matter what background or religion they were born into.

Objection: Is it true that all Jews are going to hell because they rejected Jesus?

Answer: Firstly, it is important to remember that in the first Century most believers in Jesus were Jews. But the real issue is not whether a person is Jewish or Gentile. The real issue is that Jesus provided the only atonement for our sins. Actually, more Gentiles will go to hell for rejecting Jesus than Jews, simply because there are more Gentiles in the world than Jews. Remember, all of Jesus' early disciples were Jews. And thousands of Jews in the world today believe that Jesus is the Messiah, and more are added every day.

Objection: Won't we as Jews lose our personal and national identity as Jews if we all become Christians?

Answer: Jews who embrace Yeshua as Messiah don't become Christians in the cultural sense which is really what Jewish people are asking; they become fulfilled or completed Jews by becoming disciples of Yeshua. Unfortunately the term Christian is overused and in the Jewish mind it often means someone who hates Jews and even blames them for killing Christ. Jews should certainly maintain their identity and culture as Jews after receiving Jesus as their Messiah. By doing so, we will be a more powerful and credible witness to the Jewish community than if we just blended anonymously into the Christian community. And we will add richness to the body of Messiah by helping our fellow messianic Jews to embrace their Jewish roots.

Objection: Are you telling me that a religious Jew who lives a good life and is sincere will go to hell if he doesn't believe in Jesus?

Answer: No one, no matter how good and sincere he or she may be, can take care of his or her own sin problem. We all have sinned. Only the blood of Jesus the Messiah can take away our sin. Jesus told the Jewish leaders of his day that if they didn't believe that he was who he said he was, they would die in their sins (John 8:24). This doesn't apply only to Jews, but to anyone who does not believe that Jesus is who He claims to be: the promised Messiah of Israel and the Son of the living God.

Objection: Jews believe it is blasphemy for a man to claim that he is God, and it is certainly blasphemy for us to worship a man.

Answer: You're absolutely right. It would be blasphemy for a man to claim to be God. But Jesus was not a man who claimed to be God. Rather, God came to earth in human form. Jesus didn't become God; he always was God. Isaiah 9:6 says, "For unto us a Child is born, unto us a Son is given, and the government will be upon His shoulder. And His name will be called … Mighty God, Everlasting Father." Clearly, the Messiah had to come in the form of man ("a Child is born"). Yet this child, who was thought to be only human, was also called "Mighty God" and "Everlasting Father," terms reserved for God alone.

Micah 5:2 predicted that the Messiah would be born in Bethlehem and come from the tribe of Judah. It also says, "Yet out of you [Bethlehem] shall come forth to Me the One to be Ruler in Israel, whose goings forth are from of old, from everlasting." Since no human being is "from everlasting," this passage clearly establishes that the Messiah will be God manifest in the flesh.

There is a huge difference between a man claiming to be God and God coming to earth and taking on the form of a man. Messiah is divine, God in the flesh. Christians and messianic Jews do not worship any man, but God alone.

Of course this list of objections is by no means comprehensive, but it gives you some ammunition to work with to cover the main bases. For more information on how to answer Jewish objections to the gospel, check out Dr. Michael Brown's five-book series called Answering Jewish Objections to Jesus, which is a tremendous resource and goes into a lot of detail.

KEEP TO THE BASICS

If you stick with the three principles I mentioned (original sin, the need for blood atonement, and the messiahship of Jesus), and answer every Jewish objection to the gospel as best you can in love and humility, you can help Jewish people come to Jesus. The pure simplicity and power of the gospel will win them to the Lord.

In much of the Western world, only a minority of Jews would consider themselves to be orthodox or actively practicing Judaism. In most cases, as a Bible-believing Christian, you will know far more about the Bible, even the Old Testament, than the Jews you speak to. Most Jews don't really know what they believe when it comes to Jesus, other than being taught their whole lives that Jews don't believe in him. Thankfully, due to this end-time move of the Holy Spirit, people can no longer categorically make this claim, as more Jews are coming to know their Messiah on a daily basis.

HIS BLUEPRINT WORKS

God's blueprint for the Great Commission is to take the gospel to the Jew first and then to the Gentile (Romans 1:16), not because he shows favoritism but because he knows this is the most effective method for bringing the gospel to a lost and dying human race. Because he has entrusted us with the only eternal solution to the condition of mankind, he has provided us with a pattern to do so. If we follow this simple but divinely ordained pattern in obedience, we will be amazed at the results God brings to us, our ministries, and our churches.

When I share the truth of God's blueprint all over the world, people are often filled with a passion to help reach the Jews with the gospel. Many of them don't know many Jews because they do not live in a Jewish area. Or they feel inadequate for the task. Yet they have a deep desire to make a difference among the Jewish people.

Every believer can play a role in reaching the Jews in one or more of the following ways:

1. Pray

All believers can regularly pray for the peace of Jerusalem and petition the Lord to remove the veil from the Jewish people. Prayer is the most powerful weapon we possess.

2. Give

We can donate a portion of our finances to ministries that have a proven track record of effectively reaching the Jews with the gospel. The Bible says, "You will know them by their fruits" (Matthew 7:16), so look at the fruit of any ministry you are considering donating to. Don't be afraid to ask for financial statements. More important, ask if they have testimonies of Jews coming to faith through their ministry.

3. Preach

If you feel called to share the gospel with Jewish people firsthand, do whatever you can to get fully equipped. Memorize and put into practice the principles in this book. And dig into the prophecies yourself, "rightly dividing the word of truth," so you can be a "worker who does not need to be ashamed" (2 Timothy 2:15). Ultimately, we are all called to become disciples. However we choose to do it, we should develop regular Bible reading and study habits.

The Word of God will never return void; it shall accomplish what God pleases (Isaiah 55:11). So don't get discouraged in your efforts. Share the Word with confidence and conviction, whether or not you initially see fruit. You might not be able to tell at the time how the Holy Spirit is going to use your words, but he will. So, as Winston Churchill once said, "Never, never, never, never give up."[12] As you continue to sow in faith and water your seed with prayer, you will undoubtedly reap a harvest.

---

[12]BrainyQuote.com, Xplore Inc., 2014. http://www. brainyquote.com/citation/quotes/quotes/w/winstonchu143691. html#bfXldZE8LZoiBhlC.99, accessed February 26, 2014.

PART FIVE

BLOODGUILT

All of these truths about Israel and the Jewish people and the importance of reaching them with the gospel are directly from the Scriptures and reflect the heart of God for His Chosen people. But these truths are not just for information. They are light from the Word of God and demand a response from us. With light and truth comes accountability. If you are a born again child of God and you know that Jesus is the promised Messiah and the only way to God for the Jews and for all people, it leaves you and me to respond appropriately.

The Webster's Dictionary definition of bloodguilt is "being guilty of murder or bloodshed." I wrestled with how to title this chapter on our responsibility as Christians to bring the gospel to the Jewish people. I wanted to choose a softer, more palatable heading, such as "Being a watchman for Israel." But the more I thought about it, the more I realized what a serious topic this is.

I thought back to about 1987, when I was only about three and a half years in the Lord and how the Lord first brought the reality of this subject to my attention. I had a friend whom we will call Daniel. We were very close through my teenage years while at the private Jewish School we both attended. He was about two years older than me and he was very religious, much more Orthodox in practice than I was. Daniel was, and is, an incredible Kantor with a voice second to none. He has been a full-time Rabbi or a Chazzan for practically his whole life. When I embraced Yeshua (Jesus) as my Messiah, as you can well imagine, it affected my relationship with him quite severely. Yet we have, through it all, still maintained a really strong respect for each other.

But let us go back to 1987, when this subject of bloodguilt became a reality to me. I was quite intimidated at the prospect of sharing the gospel with those more educated in the Hebrew Scriptures and more established in Judaism than I ever was. But I knew that this was no excuse for not sharing the gospel with them and that I was responsible before God for the knowledge that I had. I knew if I did not, probably no one else would. I had found out that it is extremely rare for any Christian to even attempt to share the gospel with Orthodox Jews. God had given me that burden and responsibility and I knew I could delay no longer.

So one Saturday on Shabbat I decided to arrive at the Orthodox Synagogue in Johannesburg where Daniel was the Chazzan and he was conducting a Bar Mitzvah that morning at the Shabbat service. He was pleasantly surprised to see me arrive and there were many of his friends with him, all very Orthodox, wearing mostly black, dressed like the Chabad Rabbis or in Chassidic clothing. All he had told them was that I was with him at King David High School and that I was very funny, not funny as in strange, but funny as far as having a great sense of humor. We would often joke and tease each other when we were close before I became a believer, so this is how he remembered me.

So he invited me to join him at his home with all his Orthodox friends for lunch after the Bar Mitzvah and Shabbat service ended. I readily accepted but with some trepidation, knowing in my spirit this could be quite an intense Shabbat lunch.

There were about twelve of us coming for lunch, all ranging from Orthodox to Ultra Orthodox, with one exception—me! At the time I was traveling with a team that was preaching the gospel mostly to indigenous Africans throughout South Africa and even in Swaziland. We were seeing many saved and also many healings and signs and wonders; it was a precious season. Before the others arrived for lunch I was sitting in my friend Daniel's living room as I had walked there directly from the Synagogue. One of his guests, who was very Orthodox and dressed in black, arrived a little after me and decided to sit down and chat.

All he remembered about me was that I went to the same Jewish School as Daniel and that I was very funny. So he sat down to talk to me and opened up the conversation with "small talk." After a few minutes of light conversation the subject came up as it often does in Jewish conversation, "So what do you do for a living?"

I had somehow hoped that this question would not come up at all because I knew the direction it would take us. I was only about three years in the Lord and all these guys were extremely intelligent and highly educated, not only in Judaism but in their professional fields as well. Additionally, they were all fluent or almost fluent in Hebrew and very knowledgeable of the Hebrew texts in the original language. Not only that, but I was outnumbered about twelve to one! I think after this question my heart leaped up into my throat and my neck was now beating like my heart had moved there and come to stay; at least it felt that way to me. The inevitable had happened and it seemed there was no way out.

My mind was racing, I considered all my options to avoid telling him the obvious, that I was preaching the gospel full time. I thought of maybe telling him that I was traveling through Africa with some friends, taking a few months off work to see more of the beauty of South Africa. It seemed like I did not answer for an eternity, but it was probably only about five seconds. I was sitting on the sofa, leaning forward with my elbows resting on my legs and my hands clasped together. I looked down for a moment as if in deep thought, and all of a sudden, for a brief second something happened that shook me to the core of my being. I saw both of my hands covered in blood, it was clear and bright red and flashed before my eyes. I was already quite familiar with the scriptures and as I had this vision, I immediately thought of Ezekiel chapter three. I was seeing a vision of the application of this scripture directly from the Holy Spirit.

My mind went straight to Ezekiel 3:18–19. "When I say to the wicked, 'You shall surely die,' and you give him no warning, nor speak to warn the wicked from his wicked way, to save his life, that same wicked man shall die in his iniquity; *but his blood I will require at your hand.* Yet, if you warn the wicked, and he does not turn from his wickedness, nor from his wicked way, he shall die in his iniquity; *but you have delivered your soul"* [emphasis added]. I knew immediately and without any hesitation that I would be completely honest and open about who I am, what I am doing, and I would end up sharing the gospel. I also knew that all hell was about to break loose after such a quiet and peaceful morning in the Shabbat service and the precious Bar Mitzvah we had seen. But this was such a small price to pay rather than having to face the God of Israel with blood on my hands! I didn't care what the consequences would be at this point, as long as I was right with God and obeyed Him!

I heard myself clearly answering, as if it were the most normal thing for a young Jewish man from an Orthodox Jewish background to say, in answer to his question.

"I preach the gospel."

He laughs uncomfortably. "No, seriously, what do you do for a living?"

"No, really, I preach the gospel throughout South Africa, mostly in the villages, but also in Swaziland."

"Ha ha, Daniel was right, you really are funny. That is really hysterical!"

You have to understand, in those days in South Africa it was almost unheard of for a Jew to believe in Jesus, let alone to be preaching the gospel full time. He genuinely believed that I thought up the most outlandishly crazy, funny thing I could think of just to shock him and to prove that Daniel was right about how funny I was. He continued to try to bring the conversation back to reality!

"Ok, so now seriously, what do you really do for a living?"

"No, really, I preach the gospel full time…."

Awkward silence …

"You are actually serious? You're really not joking?"

"I couldn't possibly be more serious, I believe that Yeshua (Jesus) is the promised Messiah of Israel, but not only for Israel and all the Jewish people, but for all the Gentiles as well, so I preach the gospel to whoever will listen."

He looks at me incredulously as if I had just punched him in the stomach. I looked at his face and saw a strange combination of shock, dismay and anguish. I think he was hoping that my strange sense of humor and this awkward trick I was playing with his mind might come to an end at any time. I stayed as serious as ever and looked directly in his eyes. He nervously met my gaze and it finally dawned on him that I was serious as could be. There was no turning back now, the others began to come in and take their seats at the table for lunch. There was still a stunned silence between my new friend and me!

We all took our seats and then Daniel came in. We discussed what a lovely Bar Mitzvah it was and how great the service was. I told Daniel that I still considered him to have the best voice of any Chazzan I had ever heard; I still feel that way. When he sings and chants from the Torah it feels like he is connecting directly with God and singing right from his heart. Even though he does not yet know his Messiah, I believe his heart is towards the God of Israel.

After more small talk and the Hebrew blessings over the meal, there was some hushed whispering going around the table and I could feel the tension in the room. Not that my faith was a secret, but Daniel who was not only a Chazzan but also a respected Rabbinical scholar had not told them I was a believer in Yeshua (Jesus) as Messiah. I guess he had hoped the subject would not come up or maybe that it was just a phase I was going through and the phase was now over. It has now been a 35-year "phase" and growing stronger!

I was the only guy not dressed in black with a white shirt, I felt conspicuously aware that I was the only non – Orthodox Jew in the room and possibly the first Messianic Jew many of them had ever met face to face. One of them spoke directly to me.

"So what is all this talk about believing in Jesus? Your friend Daniel is a Chazzan and you went to King David High School together, you were raised in Judaism, and you are a Cohen. How could you turn your back on your people and join the religion that has murdered millions of our people over the centuries? Our people have died as martyrs for their faith in the one true God and you just voluntarily convert!"

I responded:

"I do not consider myself to have converted and I have never
turned my back on my people. In fact, I feel more Jewish since I
have embraced our Messiah than I have ever felt before in my life.
I would never have embraced Yeshua if I did not believe with all
my heart and my soul that he is indeed the promised Messiah that
we have been waiting for."

Another guy said:

"If he was the Messiah then the Rabbis would believe in him
too; how come there is no world peace if Messiah has come? If
anything there have been even more wars in the name of religion
since Jesus came. The scripture is clear that the swords will be
beaten into plowshares when Messiah comes and the lion will lie
down with the lamb and the nations will make war no more."

I responded:

"Yes, that is true, the scripture does say that and that is
something that the Messiah will accomplish as prophesied. But
that will be at the second coming of Yeshua, what many of you
believe will be the first coming. He will return to Jerusalem
and his feet will touch down on the Mount of Olives and the
Mountain will split in two according to Zechariah 14. At that
time he will destroy Israel's enemies and establish the Messianic
Kingdom for one thousand years. But first he wants to bring
peace to our hearts. He wants to bring peace to our world before
he can bring world peace. This is what he did at his first coming
when he died for the sins of Israel and for all the Gentiles on the
cross!"

Another responded:

"You are talking about that "suffering servant" in Isaiah 53 that
Christians claim is talking about Jesus. But that clearly is not
talking about Jesus or any Messiah; it is talking about the
sufferings of our people, about Israel. Any Jew who went to the
gas chambers in the holocaust could have fulfilled that prophecy.
They all went as "lambs to the slaughter," they all "did not open

their mouths." Thousands of Jews over the centuries would fit into that description."

I responded:
"But it also says in Isaiah 53:8, 'For the transgressions of my people He was stricken.' Since when does the scripture teach that Israel can atone for her own sins through her own suffering? It was always through an animal sacrifice, by the blood of a bull or a sheep that our sins were forgiven."

Another responded:
"There have been many debates on this prophecy over the centuries between Christians and Jews and we always win the debates: you have to look into the original Hebrew context to really understand this properly."

We went back and forth a lot concerning the prophecies and what they meant in the Hebrew and the context in which they were written. But I knew the Holy Spirit had given me His wisdom to challenge them with the truth. I remembered the words of Jesus where He said, "Anyone who chooses to do the will of God will find out whether my teaching comes from God or whether I speak on my own" (John 7:17 NIV).

I said, "Look, we can debate on this subject day and night, but in the end I have one main question to challenge you all with!" Everyone became quiet and you could have heard a pin drop in the room.

"I want to ask you all one question. I know you obviously don't at this point believe that Yeshua is the Messiah of Israel. But if you knew beyond any shadow of a doubt that he was and is the Messiah would you be willing to follow Him? I say this because I know that obviously as observant Jews in South Africa we all know that we will have to pay a high price for confessing him as we will be kicked out of the synagogue and be rejected by the Jewish community at large. I know this from personal experience."

There was an awkward silence for what seemed like an eternity but in reality it was really only about 10 seconds. But to my pleasant surprise, they all said yes, one by one. But then the last person who did not respond actually said to my face that even if he knew that Jesus was the Messiah he would not follow him. I did not know if he was just playing the devil's advocate to irritate me, but I was really shocked that he could even say such a thing.

Our whole discussion and tense debate really lasted for the whole lunch, maybe one hour or so. But at the end I knew I probably would never be invited back for lunch with them again. By the way, I say that "tongue in cheek," many of them never spoke to me again and Daniel did not speak to me for about 20 years, but now thankfully we are back in touch. They knew that this was more than just a debate. They had been confronted with the truth of the scriptures by a fellow South African Jew in no uncertain terms. I knew I had to end this lively discussion in strength and in a way that they would never forget. I was reminded again of Ezekiel chapter three and the Divine mandate to proclaim the full truth to them.

I said, "I am willing to debate any of you and spend as much time as you want with me, discussing and reviewing the Old Testament prophecies. But in the end I want to declare to you that the gospel is not a debate or a discussion, but rather it is a proclamation of truth. Whether you believe it or not I want you to know that Yeshua is our promised Messiah. I also want you to know that each one of you here today will stand before Him on the Day of Judgment and answer for what you have heard this afternoon and you will be without excuse. You won't be able to say that you did not know or did not hear. I urge you to search the scriptures for yourself with an open heart and you will see that I have spoken only the truth of our own prophets."

Understandably there was a stunned silence and palpable tension in the room. I think I had effectively ruined what was supposed to have been a light, peaceful and jovial Shabbat lunch. But I had done my Father's will and obeyed the scriptures.

The rest of the lunch is a total blur to me. Of course it ended as well as it could have under the circumstances and we awkwardly tried to talk about normal everyday matters. But God had clearly spoken and my hands were now free of any man's blood. I had declared the full truth of the gospel and that was what really mattered. Now I had to believe God that His word would take

root in their souls and ultimately they would give their hearts
to Yeshua. I had fulfilled my role; they were now one hundred
percent in His capable hands. I was now free from the blood of all
men.

ONLY AN OLD TESTAMENT CONCEPT?

Whenever I share a message as strong as this one, many
Christians would say that what I am sharing is from the Old
Testament and therefore not applicable to us under the New
Covenant. To say this would be an error in itself because we will
find that Paul the Apostle, possibly the greatest apostle of all time,
who himself brought the New Covenant to the known Gentile
world for the first time, was always guided by this principle in his
life and ministry.

The first example was in Paul's ministry in Corinth found in
Acts chapter eighteen. Paul was ministering to the Gentiles as
well as to the Jews who had just recently been kicked out of Rome
by the decree of Claudius, so in a sense many of them were Jewish
refugees in this pagan Gentile city. Paul was staying and working
with one of these Jews in exile by the name of Aquila, with his
wife Priscilla. Paul stayed in this city to preach the gospel but
during the week he worked with Aquila making tents as they were
of the same trade (Acts 18:3).

But on the Jewish Sabbath, as was always Paul's pattern, he
preached the gospel in the synagogue amongst the Jews and God
fearing Gentiles who attended.

> "And he reasoned in the synagogue every Sabbath, and persuaded
> both Jews and Greeks. When Silas and Timothy had come from
> Macedonia, Paul was compelled by the Spirit, and testified to the
> Jews that Jesus was the Christ." (Acts 18:4-5)

But unfortunately in that particular synagogue those Jews
began to oppose the gospel message. Look at the response of Paul
in the next verse. "But when they opposed him and blasphemed,
he shook his garments and said to them, "Your blood be upon
your own heads: I am clean. From now on I will go to the
Gentiles." As I have pointed out previously, this was not Paul

changing the direction of his ministry or leaving the pattern of bringing the gospel to the Jew first. He was simply speaking to those specific Jewish hecklers who opposed him on that particular day.

But notice the language that Paul uses, it is almost as if he is quoting Ezekiel the prophet directly. He says, *"Your blood be upon your own heads"* [emphasis added]. Then he adds even stronger words, he declares, *"I am clean"* (emphasis added). This statement begs us to ask the obvious question. What does he mean when he says he is clean? By obvious implication it was possible for him to not be clean or innocent of their blood in this scenario.

If it were not possible then Paul would never have declared that he was clean and innocent of their blood. While Paul does not quote Ezekiel chapter three or chapter thirty-three, it is very obvious that this principle of warning the wicked to turn from their ways was worked into the fiber of his being and was a staple of his ministry and Biblical understanding. Is it therefore possible for us as New Testament believers to not be clean, in regards to sharing the gospel to those whom God has entrusted to us?

PAUL'S FINAL WORDS TO THE ELDERS IN EPHESUS

We see a second example of this principle in Paul's ministry when he shares what the Holy Spirit had shown him would be the final admonition to the Ephesian elders before his departure from this earth.

> But none of these things move me; nor do I count my life dear to myself, so I may finish my race with joy, and the ministry which I received from the Lord Jesus, to testify to the gospel of the grace of God. And indeed, now I know that you all, among whom I have gone preaching the kingdom of God, will see my face no more. Therefore I testify to you this day that I am innocent of the blood of all men. For I have not shunned to declare to you the whole counsel of God" (emphasis added).

A WORD OF ADMONITION

Again, we come to the same conclusion by implication if Paul had not declared to these elders the whole counsel of God;

he would not have been innocent of the blood of all men. The question that then arises in my mind for us is this, have we lost our conscience and sense of accountability before God to declare His full counsel just because we live in the twenty-first century?

More specifically, have we lost the admonition from God that each one of us are commanded to preach the gospel to the world beginning with the Jew according to Romans 1:16? In effect we are called to preach that there is a Day of Judgment awaiting all men because of sin, the penalty being eternal separation from God in hell. But the good news is that no one has to go there because Jesus paid the price for us all on the cross and rose from the dead. We can have forgiveness in this life and bliss in heaven for eternity instead of eternal separation from God.

There are Christian groups that love and support Israel and the Jews. At least one of them has three and a half million members. While it is refreshing and thankfully a huge change from Christian groups that are anti Semitic, I do have one fundamental bone to pick with this movement. The one thing that most of these Israel supporting groups do not do or teach is to obey the command to bring the gospel to the Jewish people.

In fact most of the bigger, better known movements are against what they would call proselytizing or converting Jews.

A few of the better known groups that operate in Israel, if you want to join their staff, you have to sign a contract wherein you agree not to share the gospel or proselytize. A leader of one such Christian group boasted in an email that in 18 years of friendship with Orthodox Jews she had never tried to proselytize or share the gospel with any of them. I was horrified; it should be a source of embarrassment and shame, not a source of boasting before men.

To boast about never proselytizing would be the equivalent to this scenario. If you knew people who were going to go aboard the Titanic and you had Divine foreknowledge through a vision or dream that the ship was going to sink but you intentionally did not forewarn them and then they drowned when the ship sank. But instead of warning them not to get on the ship, you proudly boasted afterwards that you knew that the ship would sink but never told anyone and so as a result they drowned. When people ask the obvious question as to why you did not warn them, you replied that you did not want them to worry about anything but rather you just wanted them to enjoy themselves and have a stress free vacation. So at least they could be happy in their deception of being on the safest ship ever built until it was too late and the ship hit an iceberg and they quickly sank to their destruction beneath the ocean.

Maybe your response is that this is crazy and you would never do that. But this is what millions of Christians who say that they love Israel are currently doing. My Jewish people are in effect upon this huge ship that is leading them to what Yeshua calls the wide road to destruction (Matthew 7:13). The only way off that road is onto the ship or Ark with the name Jesus. But only a handful of faithful Jewish and Gentile believers are warning them that they are on a ship that is headed towards a huge iceberg and sure destruction.

Most amazingly, those who are quiet concerning the gospel call this love. Because we don't want to potentially offend them we would rather let them go to hell because maybe they would not like us anymore if we share the gospel with them. What we are saying is that it is more important to us that our Jewish friends like us than that their souls are saved. This is in reality the highest form of selfishness. When we are quiet because we don't want to offend man, we end up offending God. The Bible says that the fear of man is a snare (Proverbs 29:25).

THE BIG LIE

My wife Tetiana and I have the honor and privilege of traveling across the world and of living and laboring amongst Jewish people in the Ukraine, South Africa, Italy and across the USA and wherever the Lord sends us. We are completely open with all our Jewish friends about Jesus. We proclaim Him as the promised and prophesied Messiah of our people and as the only way to be saved. We have found consistently that whether they accept Jesus as Messiah in the beginning or not, many of them have become our closest and most loyal friends. We are regularly in touch and sometimes we will visit them and even live in their homes for a few days or a week at a time. We share the scriptures with them and their Jewish friends from house to house and they often beg us to come back again.

I believe this is because we are open and honest about our intentions from the beginning. They know that we want them to be saved but that we love and accept them whether they accept Jesus or not. In other words, our love for them is unconditional. The big lie is that if we share the gospel with Jewish people they will all reject us and never want to be our friends again. We have found in most cases the opposite is actually the truth.

When people use what they call "friendship evangelism" with Jewish people this often backfires. In this philosophy we are just to be their friend and not share the gospel for a few years until the "right time," which is hopefully before they die without Jesus. The reason that this is rarely effective is because it often breaks trust completely. Because Jewish people often feel that this is deceptive and not honest as there is an ulterior motive. Over my thirty-five years of Jewish ministry I have found that what usually builds strong trust is when we are open about our intentions from the very beginning but have a relationship of unconditional love. I don't find any examples in the New Testament of this kind of evangelism where the gospel is not shared with a Jewish or Gentile person but a friendship is formed over many years and then the gospel is eventually shared. All of Paul's missionary journeys involve the preaching of the gospel in every city immediately first to the Jews in the synagogue and then to the Gentiles in the marketplace or from home to home.

NO CONDEMNATION

To go back to the opening point that bloodguilt according to Webster's Dictionary is being guilty of murder or bloodshed. I realize these are strong words and I am sure that most of us reading this would never be guilty of murder or bloodshed in the literal sense. But as in the example of the people going onto the Titanic, if we knew it would sink and we never warned them, we are indirectly guilty of their bloodshed or deaths because we could have prevented it if we had warned them.

So, it is the same in the spiritual world, we have the words of eternal life that can save our Jewish and Gentile friends from an eternity in hell. While we are not responsible for their final decision we are responsible to share the truth in love and to warn them about the consequence of rejecting their Messiah.

I know when I share a strong message like this Christians often say it is condemning but there is no condemnation for those who are in Christ Jesus (Romans 8:1). What you feel is conviction of truth, not condemnation. But this message is not about us who are already saved; it is about those who don't yet have the privilege of knowing Jesus and knowing that their names are written in the Lamb's Book of Life.

CONCLUSION

The time is short; the coming of the Lord is at hand. He is preparing His bride for His coming and He is calling the lost sheep of the House of Israel back to himself. You and I have the incredible honor of bringing the gospel back to those through whom it first came. Hard times lie before us and especially for the Jewish people as the tide of anti- Semitism is rising across the globe and especially in Europe, but now even in the USA, which traditionally has been so loyal to Israel and the Jews.

The scripture says, "Open your mouth wide and I will fill it" (Psalm 81:10). When your heart is full of love for the Jewish people and you share the words of eternal life with them, they will know that you love them. I am not saying that all of them will be saved. But you will be pleasantly surprised at the results and you will see with your very eyes that the Word of God never returns void. As the scriptures say, "Freely you have received, freely give" (Matthew 10:8 NIV). You have received the greatest gift that there is, the gift of free salvation and eternal life in Jesus. Don't be selfish with the gospel, don't hide your light under a bushel (Matthew 5:15 KJV).

To sum up, how can we not be guilty of bloodguilt and be able to say like Paul, "I am clean and innocent of the blood of all men?" Of course every Christian is not responsible for the preaching to the whole world. But each one of us has a sphere of influence, both Jews and Gentiles that God has placed in our lives. So let us be faithful with them and God will honor us as we honor His Word by obeying the Great Commission.

So take the gospel to the world, "First to the Jew, then to the Gentile (Romans 1:16 NIV)." Once we do this, not only will we be "innocent of the blood of all men (Acts 20:26 NIV)," that God has placed in your realm but when we stand before Jesus on that Great Day and we see our Jewish and Gentile friends standing before Him by our side we will be so glad we did. Then we will hear those long awaited words of your Savior, "Well done good and faithful servant, enter into the joy of your Lord (Matthew 25:23 NIV)." I have no doubt that you will find, as I have, that reaching the Jewish people with the gospel of their Messiah is one of the most rewarding and richest experiences of your life. Enjoy the journey as you embark on this most noble of ventures!

ABOUT THE AUTHOR

Geoffrey Cohen is a Messianic Jew from South Africa who came to faith in 1984 after a dramatic encounter with the Messiah in Jerusalem. He has a passion for God and compassion for people. Geoffrey is an author, speaker, Bible teacher, and evangelist. He has been a guest of many Christian networks such as Daystar, Jewish Voice, and the 700 Club.

Geoffrey has ministered in more than 20 nations to crowds numbering up to 100,000. He has a passion to see his own Jewish people come to know their Messiah as well as other people groups who are often bypassed. Geoffrey lives in the Dallas- Fort Worth, Texas area.

You may email Geoffrey at **cohen.geoffrey63@gmail.com**. To partner with Geoffrey to effectively reach God's Chosen People around the world with the gospel, you can give online with your tax deductible donation at Modern Day Missions using the link **http://www.modernday.org/fieldworkers/geoffrey-cohen/**.

Feel free to contact Geoffrey to speak in more detail on any of the topics in this book. He is keenly aware that partnering with churches is essential to fulfill the Great Commission.

Made in the USA
Coppell, TX
04 September 2020